# Delicious in Dungeon

Ryoko Kui

5

# Delicious in Dungeon

5

Contents

# 26. Red Dragon VII

クル
KURU
(WRAP)

PHEW.

...NO MATTER HOW I PROCESS IT, WE'LL NEVER EAT IT ALL...
Boneless Dragon Hams
Red dragon thigh meat—2 kg
Seasonings————To taste

ぱち
PACHI
(BLINK)

MOZO (RUSTLE)
もぞ

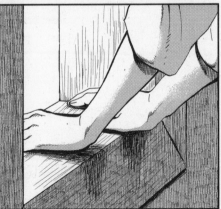

FURA (STAGGER)
フラ
FURA
フラ
HISO (WHISPER)
ヒソ
HISO
ヒソ
GYUU (SQUEEZE)
ぎゅう
GUI (TUG)
ぐい
BA (YANK)
バッ
......
......

SO THERE YOU ARE, HM?
WHAT DO YOU CALL THAT FORM?

YOU WERE TASKED WITH SEARCHING FOR HIS MAJESTY.
I DON'T RECALL RELIEVING YOU OF YOUR DUTY.

PETAN (FWUMP)
ぺたん

ガタ—ン
GATAN (CLATTER)
ビクッ
BIKU (FLINCH)

...WHAT WAS THAT?

THE SWORD WAS PROPPED UP, AND I GUESS IT FELL OVER.
HAAH...
TIE THAT THING UP ALREADY.

WHEW...

ZZZZ...

FALIN?

MARCILLE, WHERE'S FALIN?

HUH?

SENSHI, WHERE DID FALIN GO?

?
NOBODY CAME THROUGH HERE.

WHAT...? WHAT'S WRONG?

SHE CAN'T HAVE...
DID SHE LEAVE THROUGH HERE...?

...I'M GOING OUT TO LOOK FOR HER!
GU (GRAB)

BA (DASH)
LAIOS!

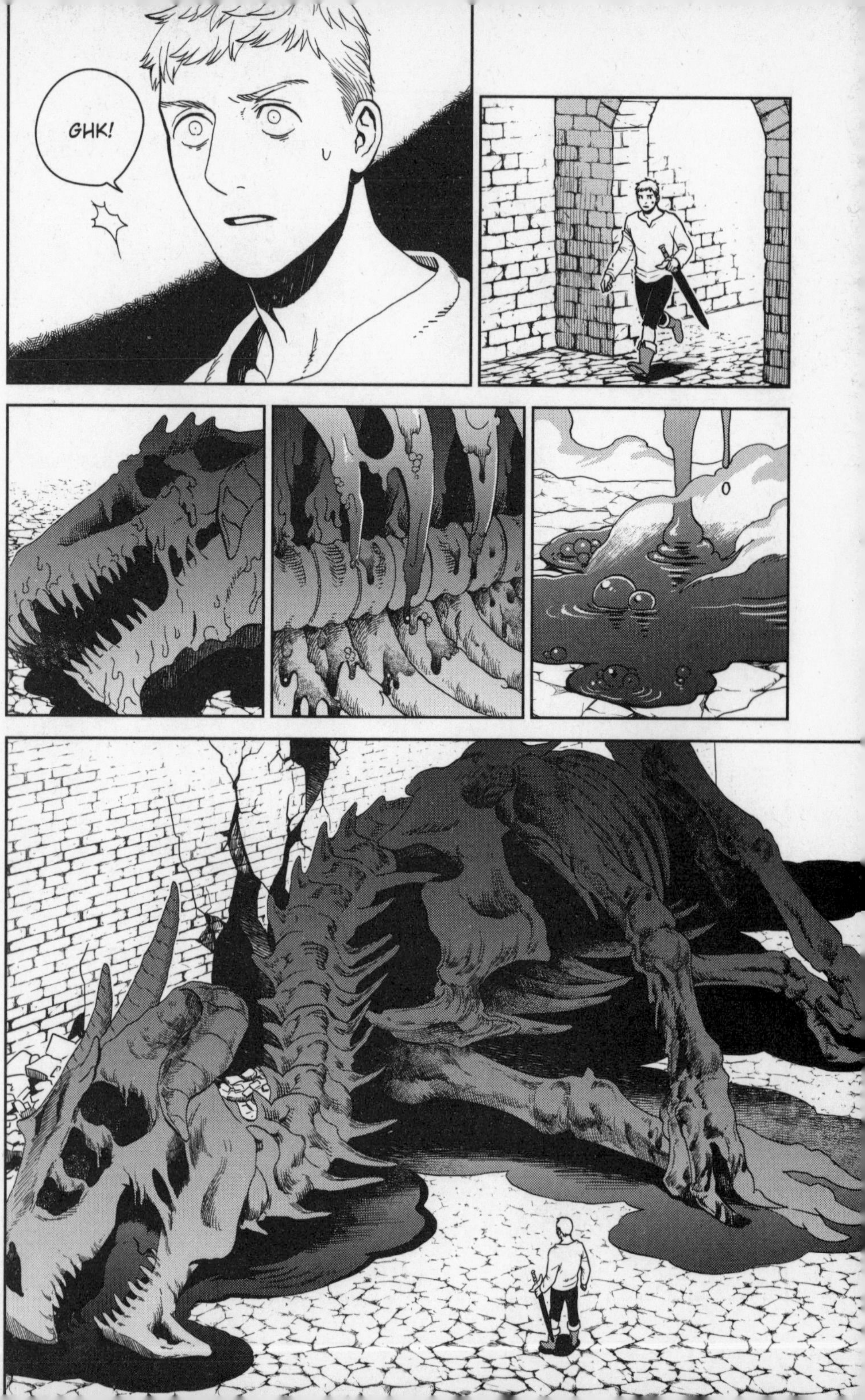

GHK!

WHAT'S THIS...?

FALIN!

ARE YOU OKAY?

カタ…
KATA (RATTLE)

WHAT ON EARTH HAPPENED?
ゴト
GOTO (THNK)
UNH...

LORD DELGAL...
ブツ
BUTSU (MUTTER)
ブツー
BUTSU
HAVE TO SEARCH...

"DELGAL"?
WHO'S...?

IN THIS LAND...
ビクッ
BIKU (FLINCH)

IN THIS LAND, ALL BUILDINGS, COINS, CITIZENS, LIVESTOCK, BLOOD, AND FLESH...
...DOWN TO EVERY GRAIN OF SAND UNDER YOUR FEET...
EVERYTHING IS THE PERSONAL PROPERTY OF HIS MAJESTY, KING DELGAL.

YOU FILTHY THIEF.

YOU...

YOU... THE LORD OF THE DUNGEON...

THE LUNATIC MAGICIAN !!

PAAN (BLAM)
BASHAN (SPLOOSH)
Y-YOU THERE! GET BACK!
A CHILD !?
THE NEXT ONE WILL HIT YOU!
......
KNOW YOUR PLACE...!

FALIN, CAN YOU STAND?
YUSA (SHAKE)
NNH...
FALIN!
—SHUT UP!!
GUA (LUNGE)
DO (WHUD)
DOSHA (FWUMP)
L-LAIOS!
WHAT STRENGTH!
WHAT'S GOING ON?
IS SHE AN ADVEN-TURER?

BA (F'WAP)

HM!?
ピク
PIKU (TWITCH)
A BOOK!?

I'VE GOT A REALLY BAD FEELING...

PULL YOURSELF TOGETHER, LAIOS.

HMMM !?
HEY. SHE'S CASTING SOME-THING.
THAT CHANT...

ZOWA (SHIVER)
ANCIENT MAGIC.

ぬう
NUU
(ZLOOP)

ゴポポッ
GOPO
(BLUP)

DEVOUR THEM!!
BA

HUH!?

AH!
BI (SNIK)
DOSHA (WHUMP)
EXPLO-SIVE SPELLS.
DEFENSE SPELLS...
NO. THOSE WON'T BLOCK THEM.
IN THAT CASE...
GUI (WIPE)
GYUU (SQUEEZE)
MISHI (KRIKL)
MISHI
...I'LL OVERWRITE THE SPELL DIRECTLY!!

SUU (SHUF)
スーッ…

BISHI
ビシ
BISHI (KSHH)
ビシッ

RELEASE!!
PASHAA (SPLAAASH)
パシャーッ
BISHA (SPLISH)
ビシャッ

ピク
PIKU (TWITCH)

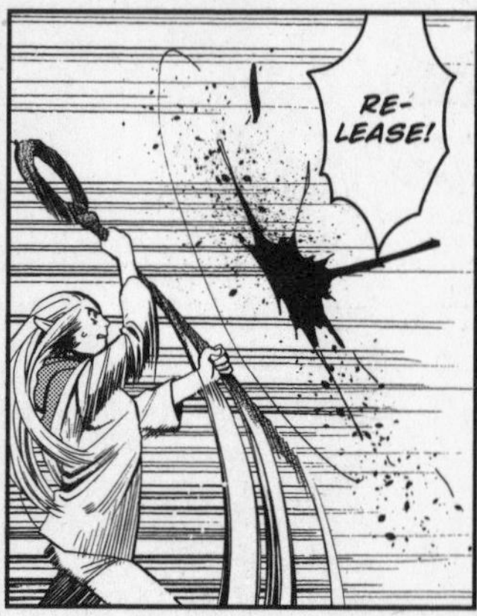
RE-LEASE!

RE-LEASE!

RE-LEASE!!!

PA (POP)
YEEEG...!
PA
PA

PA
THIS ANCIENT MAGIC...
I UNDERSTAND IT! I CAN READ IT!
PA

UU! HEE-HEE!
BUT...
...I CAN'T KEEP UP WITH IT!!

BONELESS DRAGON HAMS
Red dragon thigh meat—2 kg
Seasonings——To taste

BONELESS DRAGON HAMS
Red dragon thigh meat—2 kg
Seasonings——To taste

HAGK!
HAFF!

HFF...
Y-YOU MADE THIS DUNGEON ...?
I...
HFF...
...WANT TO TALK TO Y—
GURA (LURCH)

GAPAA (GAPE)
HUH!?

WAAAAH!!

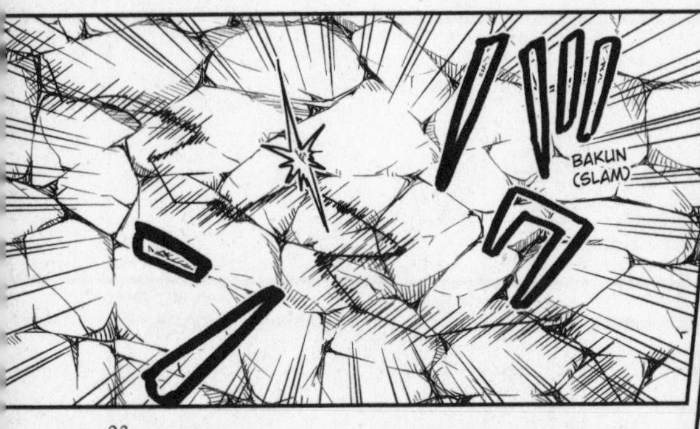
BAKUN (SLAM)

PATAN (SHUT)
パタン
HMPH.

SETTLE DOWN.
SU (SWISH)
スッ
THE REBELS ARE GONE.

......

HIS MAJESTY WILL RETURN SOON TOO.
にこっ
NIKO (SMILE)
WHEN HE DOES, LET'S HAVE A GRAND CELEBRA-TION.

......

ビク
BIKU (FLINCH)
HEY.
DRAGON.

THAT'S INCON-VENIENT, ISN'T IT?
I'LL GIVE YOU A NEW SHAPE.

ボコッ
BOKOKO (BLURBLE)

ボコッ
BOKO (BLORP)
ボッ
BOKO

CARRY OUT YOUR DUTY.

......
I WILL...

......

NH...
GOSO (RUSTLE)
ゴソ...
OW...

WHAT'S GOING ON?
HANG ON. I'LL MAKE A LIGHT...

PO (GLEAM)
ポッ
PO
ポッ

POO
ポオ

WHAT IS THIS PLACE?
WHERE DID WE FALL IN FROM...?

WHAT'S GOING ON?
KO KO (TAP)
THE EXIT'S...?

ZU (RUMBLE)

ZU
ZU
WAAH!?
WHAT IS THAT!?
ZU
HUH? I THINK THE WALLS ARE CLOSING IN!!
ZU
ZU
YOU'VE GOTTA BE KIDDING! DAMMIT!
ZU
EXIT! FIND AN EXIT!!
ZU
CAN'T YOU DO SOMETHING WITH MAGIC!?
WHAT KIND OF MAGIC, EXACTLY!?

ZO (SHIVER)
WE'RE GOING TO DIE.

IT'S NOT THE FIRST TIME, BUT...
...NOBODY WILL FIND US IF WE'RE BURIED IN ROCK.

WE FINALLY FOUND FALIN.
I WAS SO CLOSE TO THE DUN-GEON'S MYSTERY.
...AND NOW IT WON'T MEAN A THING.

JIWA (TEARY)
FOR IT TO END THIS WAY IS JUST...

HIYA (CHILL)

HUH...?

GU (CLAMP)
MMPH!!

MMPH !!?

MARCILLE !?

SUPPON (POP)

I-IT'S A CAVE!!
WE CAN GET OUT THAT WAY!

WE DON'T KNOW WHERE IT GOES.
ANYTHING'S BETTER THAN BEING FLATTENED!!
JUST GO! HURRY!

ボフッ
BOFU (FWUMP)

WHERE ARE WE?
...IT'S COLD!

F-FOR NOW, WE'VE GOT TO GET OUT OF HERE.

...CAN'T.
I CAN'T BOOVE A VINGER EDDY BORE...

NO, TRY HARDER.
IF SHE FINDS US AGAIN...

IT'S...
IT'S ALL OVER.

30. Good Medicine

SFX: BOSO (MUTTER) BOSO

TH-THEY VANISHED.
AGH, DAMMIT, I'M GOING TO GO CRAZY.
SENSHI, WAKE UP LAIOS.
I'LL GO SEE WHAT IT'S LIKE OUT THERE.

GIII (CREAK)
ギィ…

QUIET DOWN!
WHAT'S GOING ON!?
MOLES, CAPTAIN.
HOW DID THEY GET IN?
WHAT WERE THE GUARDS DOING?
THE HOLE CLOSED UP.
A DEPTHS-DWELLER.
A LITTLE MAN.
GWEH!
A LONG-LEGS, AND...
...A LONG-EARS!

INTER-ESTING.
I'VE NEVER KILLED A LONG-EARS BEFORE.
I'LL DO IT.
GIVE THE LITTLE MAN TO THE DOGS.
GRRR...
THEY'RE STARVED FOR ENTERTAIN-MENT.
KUN KUN (SNIFF)

WAIT.
AREN'T YOU CHIEF ZON'S YOUNGER SISTER?

WE CAME HERE TO KEEP A PROMISE TO THE CHIEF.
I REQUEST LENIENCE.

HOW DO YOU KNOW THAT NAME?

...HM!?

KUN
KUN
KUN

ARE YOU THE VEGETA-BLE SELLER !?
WA (CLAMOR)
WE DIDN'T RECOGNIZE YOU. YOU SMELL DIFFERENT.
THE BATH ...!!

TO THINK YOU'D COME ALL THE WAY HERE...
WHAT DID YOU PROMISE THE CHIEF?

I THANK YOU IN THE CHIEF'S PLACE.
ONE OF YOU, PREPARE FOR COMPOUNDING.

SO THAT'S WHAT HAPPENED.
I THOUGHT IT WAS ODD THAT THE DRAGON WAS SUDDENLY GONE.

...I SEE.

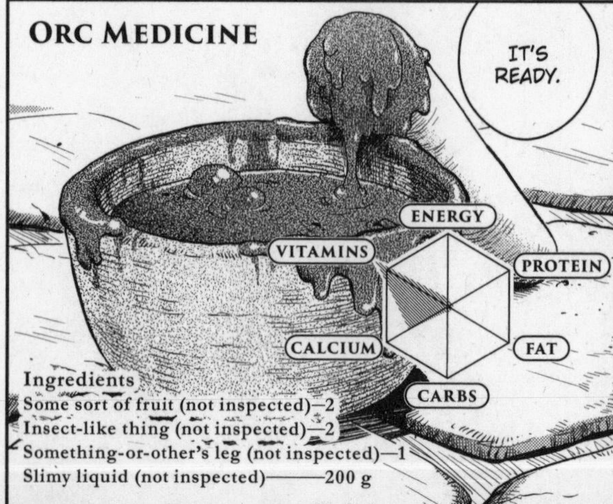
ORC MEDICINE
IT'S READY.
ENERGY
VITAMINS
PROTEIN
CALCIUM
FAT
CARBS
Ingredients
Some sort of fruit (not inspected)—2
Insect-like thing (not inspected)—2
Something-or-other's leg (not inspected)—1
Slimy liquid (not inspected)———200 g

GORI (GRIND)
GORI

GOBU (SPLURT)
ごぶ

GUI (SHLURP)
ぐい

KON (TAP)
KON
BLEH...

BIKU
BIKUN (THRASH)
NNNNNNH!!!

HNFFF!
...NA...
HNFFF!

I...
I...I'M JUSH...
...OUD OF MA...

S-SAY...
WE WERE ATTACKED BY AN ELF MAGICIAN.
DO YOU KNOW ANYTHING ABOUT HER?

YOU MET HER!?
ZUI (LOOM)
AGH!?

UM.
BROWN SKIN, SILVER HAIR...?
THAT'S THE ONE.

......
I DON'T KNOW ANY PARTIC-ULARS.

ONLY THAT SHE WAS HERE LONG BEFORE WE MOVED IN...
...AND THAT SHE'S SAID TO RULE THE DUNGEON.

IF OUTSIDERS MEDDLE WITH THE DUNGEON MORE THAN NECESSARY...
...SHE APPEARS.

SHE CREATES MON-STERS, CON-TROLS THEM...
...CHANGES THE LAY OF THE LAND...

SHE CAN KILL ANYTHING, JUST BY PAGING THROUGH A BOOK.

RULES THE DUNGEON?
YOU MEAN...

...WE CAUGHT THE ATTENTION OF THE LUNATIC MAGICIAN?
DON'T EVEN JOKE ABOUT THAT!

DID KILLING THE RED DRAGON DO IT?
DID MARCILLE'S MAGIC ATTRACT HER?
DAMMIT!
SOWA SOWA (PANIC)
WE HAVE TO GET OUT OF HERE NOW!

SHE HAS SEVERAL MONSTERS WORKING FOR HER.
IF YOU KILL THEM, YOU DRAW HER ANGER.

TO GUARD AGAINST THAT, MY BIG BROTHER TOLD US NOT TO TOUCH THE RED DRAGON.
MY BROTHER IS ALWAYS RIGHT.
THAT JERK.

WHEN THOSE TWO WAKE UP, THEY'LL WANT TO GO LOOK FOR FALIN.

WE'VE GOT TO MAKE THEM GIVE UP.
MEAN-ING...?

ANY-THING'S FINE.
WE COULD BURN HER STAFF.
OR SAY THAT WE'RE SATISFIED NOW WE'VE EATEN DRAGON MEAT.
OR THAT WE SAW FALIN SET OFF FOR THE SURFACE.
YOU MEAN TRICK THEM?
YEAH, I DO!
IF WE DON'T, THOSE IDIOTS WILL NEVER GIVE UP.

IF WE GO ANY FURTHER, WE'LL BE KILLED FOR SURE.
DO YOU WANT TO BE PART OF THE WALL?
I SURE DON'T.

THERE'S ABSOLUTELY NO WAY I'M DYING WITH THOSE TWO.

......

SAY...
I'D LIKE TO GO PICK UP THE THINGS WE LEFT.
COULD YOU SHOW US THE WAY?
HMM...
NO.
THE STINK OF YOUR ROTTEN NATURE MIGHT RUB OFF ON ME.

WHA...!?
PLEASE, I'M ASKING YOU AS WELL.
TAKE HIM THERE.

HE'S A COWARD, BUT HE ISN'T A BAD PERSON.

SENSHI! YOU'RE NOT COMING!?
SOMEBODY NEEDS TO STAY WITH THOSE TWO.

...IF YOU'RE ASKING, THEN I CAN'T ARGUE.
I DON'T LIKE IT, BUT I'LL GUIDE HIM.

DAMMIT.
THEY'RE ALL IDIOTS, EVERY LAST ONE OF THEM. IDIOTS!

SO YOU LOST A COMPANION?

...YEAH.
THE LAST TIME WE SAW HER, SHE WAS ON THE GROUND AT THE FEET OF THAT MAGICIAN.
IT'S PRETTY HARD TO BE OPTIMISTIC.

MAYBE. THAT'S NO EXCUSE FOR TRICKING YOUR COM-PANIONS.
TCH!
PRETTY EASY TO TALK WHEN IT'S NOT YOUR PROBLEM.

UH, NO.
JIRO (GLARE)
IT'S NOTHING.

BEHIND YOU.
HUH?

WH—
AGH!
BOFU (BAFF)

SUU (SWISH)
......

DON'T MAKE A FUSS.
!??
HINYARI (CHILL)
SHE'S A RESI-DENT OF THIS CITY.

THE GHOSTS AROUND HERE ARE STILL SANE.
THEY ONLY APPEAR WHEN THEY WANT TO BE SEEN.

THE PATHS THEY TRAVEL ARE SAFE.
LET'S FOLLOW HER.

FOR REAL...?

THAT'S WHERE WE WERE.
I COULD'VE SWORN WE FELL FROM THERE, BUT...
THE RED DRAGON'S GONE.

OH...!
OVER THERE.

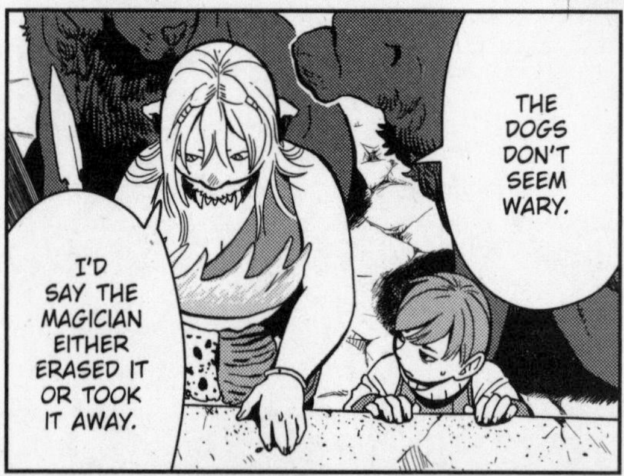
THE DOGS DON'T SEEM WARY.
I'D SAY THE MAGICIAN EITHER ERASED IT OR TOOK IT AWAY.

NO. DON'T TELL ME...
ビクッ
BIKURI (FLINCH)
DID IT... COME BACK TO LIFE!?

ONE OF OUR PARTY CAST A DEFENSIVE SPELL...

WE USED FIRE NEAR THE DRAGON'S FUEL SAC, AND IT CAUGHT.
AND YOU WERE ALL RIGHT!?

...I SEE TRACES OF AN EXPLO-SION...

...IT PROTECTED US, SO WE WERE FINE.

YOU'VE GOT SOME GOOD COMPANIONS.

THAT'S NOT THE POINT.
EVEN SHE DIDN'T KNOW SHE COULD USE THAT SPELL.

OUR HEALER CHARGED IN, AND WE WERE ALMOST BLOWN AWAY.
SURE, IT WORKED IN THE END, BUT...

...IF IT HADN'T, IT WOULD HAVE BEEN A DUMB MOVE!
THAT'S WHAT THEY'RE LIKE.

HOW DID YOU SLAY THE RED DRAGON ON YOUR OWN ANYWAY?

SENSHI AND I ACTED AS BAIT.
THEN WHEN THERE WAS AN OPENING, LAIOS GRABBED HIS CHANCE, AND—
OH, HE'S THE TALL-MAN. ANYWAY, HE...

...JUMPED RIGHT IN CLOSE AND NAILED THE DRAGON IN A VITAL SPOT.
OH-HO.

THAT'S SPLENDID.
THOSE WHO FIGHT MUST BE COURAGEOUS.

...THAT WASN'T COURAGE.
IT WAS A FOOL'S GAMBLE. WE WERE LUCKY IT WORKED.

FRANKLY, IT GAVE ME CHILLS.
IT STUCK BACK ON!
WHAT'S GOING TO HAPPEN TO A GUY WHO MAKES DECISIONS LIKE THAT?

WE HAD COMPANIONS WHO LEFT THE PARTY.
THEY MAY HAVE BEEN THE SMART ONES.

I SHOULD HAVE LEFT THEN TOO, INSTEAD OF BEING STUBBORN.

AND THAT WOULD HAVE BEEN WORTH LOSING A COMPANION?

YOU NEVER KNOW...

MAYBE HE COULDN'T TURN BACK BECAUSE I SAID I'D GO ALONG.

WHAT HAPPENED AFTER THAT?

WE HEALED OUR WOUNDS ...
...AND EVERY-THING ELSE...

GII (CREAK)
AND IN THIS ROOM, WE...

...COOKED UP THE DRAGON MEAT AND ATE IT.

THAT'S GOOD.
IT'S THE VICTORS' PRIVILEGE.
YEAH, WELL.

AND AFTER THAT, THE MAGICIAN APPEARED?
HOW DID YOU SURVIVE?

OUR MAGICIAN HELD UP UNDER THE ATTACKS.

HUH!
THE LONG-EARS WHO WAS ON THE FLOOR!?
AND SHE HAD SUCH A SILLY-LOOKING FACE...

SHE ACTUALLY IS SILLY.
SHE USES SKETCHY MAGIC TOO.
EVEN IF WE GET OUT OF THE DUNGEON, I DOUBT SHE'LL MANAGE TO LIVE A DECENT LIFE.

THEY ASSUME IF THEY PUSH THEM-SELVES, THEIR EFFORTS WILL BE REWARDED.

—TCH.
THEY'RE ALL IDIOTS, MORONS, AND HOPELESS FOOLS.

AFTER ALL, I'M A COWARD, AND MY LIFE IS WHAT'S MOST IMPORTANT TO ME!
IF LYING WILL GET US BACK TO THE SURFACE, SO BE IT!
NOT WHAT I MEANT.

SO YOU'RE TRICKING THEM!?
YOU THINK IT'S POSSIBLE TO PERSUADE PEOPLE LIKE THAT!?
THERE'S A BETTER WAY TO DO IT.

JUST BE HONEST AND TELL THEM YOU DON'T WANT THEM TO DIE.

ガッ
GA (TRIP)

...THAT LITTLE... WHY IS IT HERE?
DID IT CRAWL ALL THE WAY OVER!?

YOU WERE THE SMARTEST ONE IN THE GROUP.

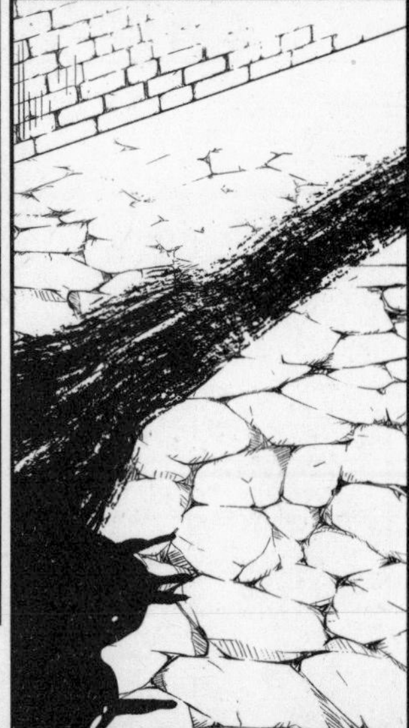

A BLOOD TRACK...
AS IF SOMEONE DRAGGED A CORPSE...

I'LL LEAVE WITHOUT YOU.
R-RIGHT.

ガチャ
GACHA (CHAK)
I GOT OUR STUFF.

WHOA!
WHAT ARE YOU DOING!?
SERI-OUSLY, REST!

ずっ
ZU (PRESS)
NOTHING HURTS.
ず
ZU
WOW.
ずっ
ZU
ONLY BECAUSE YOUR NERVES ARE SCREWY FROM THE MEDICINE.
FALIN IS STILL NEARBY. SHE HAS TO BE.

ドッ
DO (WHUD)
CALM DOWN!

HAAAH...

...I NEED TO TALK TO YOU TWO.

LET ME TALK FIRST.

SU (SHUF)
CHILCHUCK, I THOUGHT ABOUT IT, AND I...

LAIOS.
I CAN'T BEGIN TO KNOW WHAT YOU'RE FEELING RIGHT NOW.

GU (CLENCH)

SOMEBODY WILL DIE FOR SURE.

EVEN SO, AS THINGS STAND...
...WE CAN'T CONTINUE THIS EXPEDI-TION.

FOR NOW, GRIT YOUR TEETH AND GO BACK TO THE SURFACE.
I'M BEGGING YOU, LAIOS!

I DON'T WANT TO LOSE YOU GUYS!
MAYBE THEY'RE NOT AS INTENSE AS YOUR FEELINGS FOR YOUR SISTER, BUT I'VE GOT THREE PEOPLE TO THINK OF HERE.
IF WE SAY WE SAW THE LUNATIC MAGICIAN, THE LORD OF THE ISLAND MIGHT ACT!
OR WE COULD COLLECT MONEY AND HIRE SOME-BODY!
IF WE'RE BETTER PREPARED, WE CAN GET TO THIS LEVEL FASTER.

SO...
... PLEASE...
...LET'S TURN BACK, LAIOS...

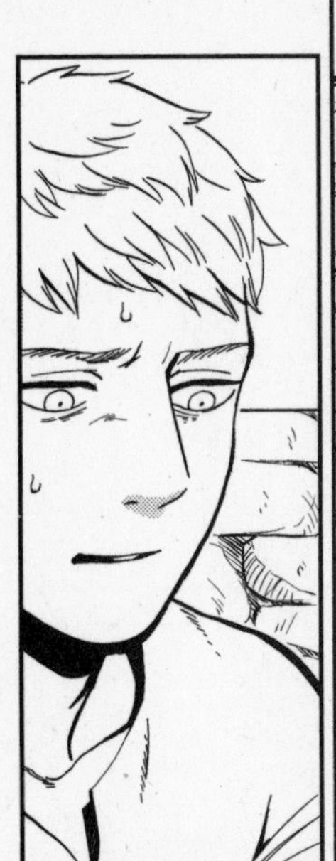

AS A MATTER OF FACT...

...WE'RE NEARLY OUT OF SOME FOODSTUFFS, SEASON-INGS AND SUCH.
I'D LIKE TO GIVE FALIN A PROPER MEAL.

WE SHOULD GO BACK TO TOWN FOR SUPPLIES.

I SENT A MESSENGER TO REPORT THE RED DRAGON'S DEATH.

MY BROTHER AND THE REST WILL RETURN SOON.
IF YOU PREPARE AND THEN COME BACK...

...WE'LL DO ALL WE CAN TO HELP YOU.

I'M SORRY FOR WORRYING YOU.
LET'S TURN BACK FOR NOW.

**Chapter 30: The End**

# 31. Sea Serpent, Part 1

A LITTLE EARLI-ER...

IS YOUR MIND CLEAR?
NOTHING PHYS-ICALLY SEEMS OFF?
I'M NOT SEEING ANY PROB-LEMS...

YOU DIDN'T HAVE ENOUGH BLOOD, SO I USED GOAT BLOOD, BUT...
...IT'S NOT A PERFECT FIX.
I'D MAKE A TRIP BACK TO TOWN.

IF YOU'D STAYED DEAD IN THE WATER, YOU'D BE FISH FOOD NOW.
UP WE GET.
BE GRATEFUL TO WHOEVER HAULED YOU OUT.

HAULED US OUT? YOU DON'T MEAN...
...
KURO!

I KNOW THIS SMELL!
SUN
SUN (SNIFF)
SUN
IT'S THE TREASURE TAKERS!
I KNEW IT! IT'S THOSE GUYS!

REVIVAL FEE.
I'LL LET YOU OFF FOR THE PRICE OF THE GOAT.

I THINK... WE WERE ATTACKED BY FISH-MEN...
GYU (SQUEEZE)
APPARENTLY, WE DIED AGAIN.

AN ADVEN-TURER ...?
YES, THAT'S ALL OF IT.

YOU'RE ...

WHAT?
... NOTHING.

LET'S GO, NAMARI.
OH. YEAH.

......
SO YOU GO FOR DWARFS TOO?
YOU HAVE NO PRINCI-PLES.

I'VE NEVER CHOSEN MY FRIENDS BASED ON HEIGHT.
IS THAT RIGHT.

EE YAA!
OUR PROVISIONS ARE GONE!
THEY TOOK THEM! AGAIN!
FOOD...

DON'T SCREW WITH ME, PEOPLE!
AGAIN ...?
PYON (BOING)
PYON

THEY LEFT THE MONEY AND JUST TOOK THE FOOD?
MAYBE THEY'D RUN OUT?
THAT BURNS ME UP...
WE'LL REALLY HAVE TO TELL THEM OFF.

WHAT DO WE DO, KABRU?
HM...

THERE'S NO HELP FOR IT.
LET'S HEAD BACK TO TOWN.

WHA—!?
ARE YOU SERIOUS!?
WITH THE CULPRITS STILL ON THE LOOSE?
WE'RE OUT OF FOOD. WE CAN'T JUST KEEP GOING.

WE HAVE TO ADMIT WE WEREN'T STRONG ENOUGH.
IT'S LIKE THOSE PEOPLE SAID.
WE SHOULD JUST BE GRATEFUL WE'RE ALIVE.

IF THAT'S YOUR DECISION, KABRU, I'LL OBEY.
ME TOO.
THANK YOU, HOLM.
DAYA.

IF YOU PROMISE WE WON'T GIVE UP ON FINDING THE CULPRITS...
...THEN I'M OKAY WITH IT.
I PROMISE, RIN.

KURO WILL FOLLOW MIKBELL.
......

HAAAAAH...

THIS EXPEDITION REALLY LEFT US IN THE RED.
SOME OF THEM DO THAT.

IT'S GOTTEN MISTY.
EVERY-BODY BE CAREF...

HM?

!

THIS ISN'T A NATURAL MIST!!
IS IT THE WORK OF A MONSTER?
HFFFH...
HFFFH...

FISH-MEN!?
HFFH!
HFF!
THERE ARE SO MANY! WHEN DID THEY...!?
HFF!
HFF!
DAMN. I'LL HAVE TO FIGHT...

HERE IT COMES!!
EEP!
GRAAAAAH!!
GIIIN (CLANG)

ビーー
BIRI (STRAIN)
GHK...!?
PYON (BOING)
ピョン
ピョン
PYON
ビリ
BIRI
THAT SLASHING, SWEEPING AX...!
HRRAAAA
RIGHT.
THIS IS...
I KNOW THAT STYLE.

GA
(WHUD)
DOBOO
(BLOOSH)
GNPAR!
SHH!
IT'S OKAY.
CALM DOWN.
DAYA. IT'S ME.
GRR...
???

THIS MIST IS ILLUSION MAGIC.

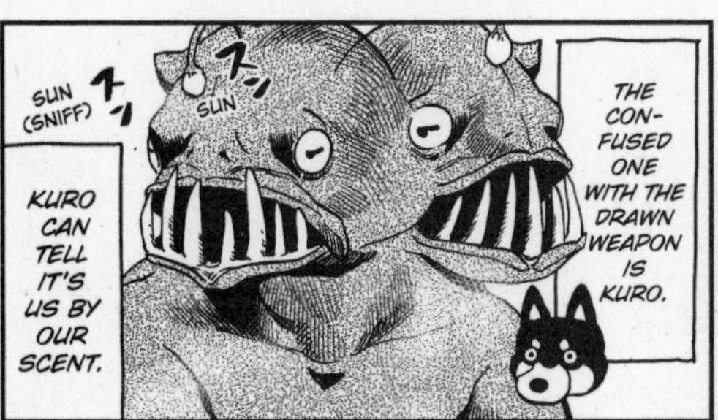
THE CON- FUSED ONE WITH THE DRAWN WEAPON IS KURO.
SUN (SNIFF)
SUN
KURO CAN TELL IT'S US BY OUR SCENT.

...
THEN I GUESS THAT SPACEY ONE IS HOLM.
HE TENDS TO FREEZE UP WHEN THINGS HAPPEN ALL AT ONCE.

THE ONE WHO RAN OFF MUST BE MIK.
SA (SWSH)
THEN THE MOST DANGER- OUS ONE NOW IS...

BUTSU
BUTSU (MUTTER)
RIN!

THERE, YOU SEE!? SHE'S CHANT- ING!
SHE COULD TURN US ALL TO CINDERS.
IF YOU WANT TO STOP A MAGICIAN'S CHANT PEACEFULLY...

RINSHA.

YOU CAN TELL, CAN'T YOU?

THIS IS AN ILLUSION.

...
IT'S TOO BAD SHE LOOKS LIKE A MONSTER.

OKAY.
IN ORDER TO STOP THIS MIST ILLUSION ...

TCH!

DA (DASH)
GO (WHUD)

WH-WHY, YOU—!

DO (THWOK)

HE'S NOT THE ONE.
CASTERS DON'T COME AT YOU WITH WEAPONS.

HE'LL BE WATCHING US FROM THE FRINGE.

THAT ONE!

WHA...
WHAT...?

AH...

BUWA (FWOOSH)
ぶわっ
AAAAAGH!

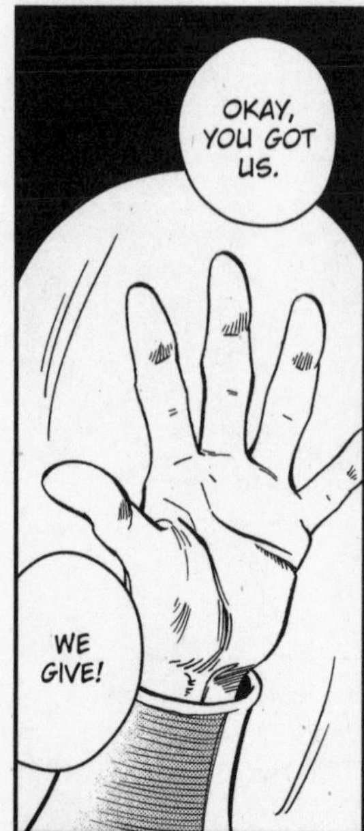
OKAY, YOU GOT US.
WE GIVE!

FU (FFT)

GYO (JOLT)
LET HIM GO, WOULDJA?

THESE GUYS...!
THEY'RE THE CORPSE RETRIEV-ERS FROM UP-STAIRS!

I DOUBT THIS WAS A CHANCE REUNION.
I BET THEY FOLLOWED US.

WH-WHAT DO YOU MEAN?
CORPSES RETRIEVED ON LOWER LEVELS ARE WORTH MORE.
IN SUBSIDIES FROM THE ISLAND.
ポン
PON (PAT)

WE GOT ALL FIRED UP TO RETAKE OUR STOLEN BOUNTY...
...AND WENT TO A LEVEL WE COULDN'T HANDLE.

THEY KNEW IF THEY FOLLOWED US FROM A DISTANCE...
VOILÀ—MORE VALUABLE CORPSES.
PUKAA (BLOOP)

AHA...
THE NERVE!

YOU WERE A LITTLE LATE, THOUGH.
BY THE TIME YOU FOUND US, WE'D BEEN REVIVED...
...AND WERE HEADING BACK TO THE SURFACE.

YOU PANICKED AND TOOK DRASTIC STEPS.
USING AN ILLUSION TO MAKE US KILL OURSELVES.

TOO BAD.
WHO'D HAVE THOUGHT YOU'D GET WIPED OUT BY MONSTERS SO SOON? HEH HEH.

CLOSE, BUT NOT QUITE.
IDEALLY, YOU WOULD HAVE CAUGHT UP TO THOSE THIEVES AND KILLED EACH OTHER.

SIGH...

THEFT AND COMBAT AMONG ADVEN-TURERS ARE GRAVE CRIMES.
WE'RE REPORTING THIS TO THE LORD OF THE ISLAND.

YOU LITTLE ...!

AS IT HAPPENS, TWO OF OUR COMPANIONS ARE OUT COLD.
TAKE THEM TO THE RESURRECTION OFFICE. THEY SHOULD PAY YOU A FAIR SUM.

WANT TO MAKE A DEAL?
IF YOU GO BACK NOW, YOU'LL LOSE OUT TOO.

THEY'RE ONLY UNCON-SCIOUS.

KURU (TWIRL)

PON (TMP)
WE'LL TESTIFY THAT THEY WERE ATTACKED BY FISH-MEN.

FOR OUR SHARE, WE'LL TAKE... LET'S SEE.
40...NO, 30 PERCENT.

WHAT DO YOU SAY?
THIS WAY, NOBODY LOSES.

......

FINE.
IT'S A DEAL.

KABRU ...

GU (LIFT)
GYUN (WHIRR)

ドッ
DO
(SHÜNK)

WHA
...!?
GOBO
(SPLRT)
ゴボ
YOU
LITTLE
...
WELL,
OF
COURSE.
THAT'S
HOW IT
SHOULD
BE!

ドボ
DOBO (SPLASH)
ダボン
DABON (SPLOOSH)

YEE... YEEEEK!

KURO, WOULD YOU GO FIND MIK?
SHE'LL BE HIDING OVER THERE.
WUFF.

THEY ALL HAVE THE SAME VITAL SPOTS.
AND THEY MOVE THE SAME WAY.
IT WOULD BE SIMPLER IF MONSTERS WERE LIKE THAT TOO.
TALL-MEN, DWARVES, AND GNOMES ...

WHEW.
PEOPLE ARE NICE AND EASY.

I DIDN'T KNOW ABOUT ANY OF THIS!
PL-PLEASE, LET ME GO!
WHAT SHOULD WE DO WITH HIM?

KABRU.

IF THIS GOES ON, EVERYONE DECENT WILL ABANDON THE ISLAND.

MORE AND MORE PEOPLE ARE MAKING THEIR LIVING STEALING FROM OTHERS.

YOU AREN'T TRYING TO BREAK THE DUN-GEON'S CURSE.
YOU DON'T WANT TO EXTERMI-NATE THE MON-STERS.

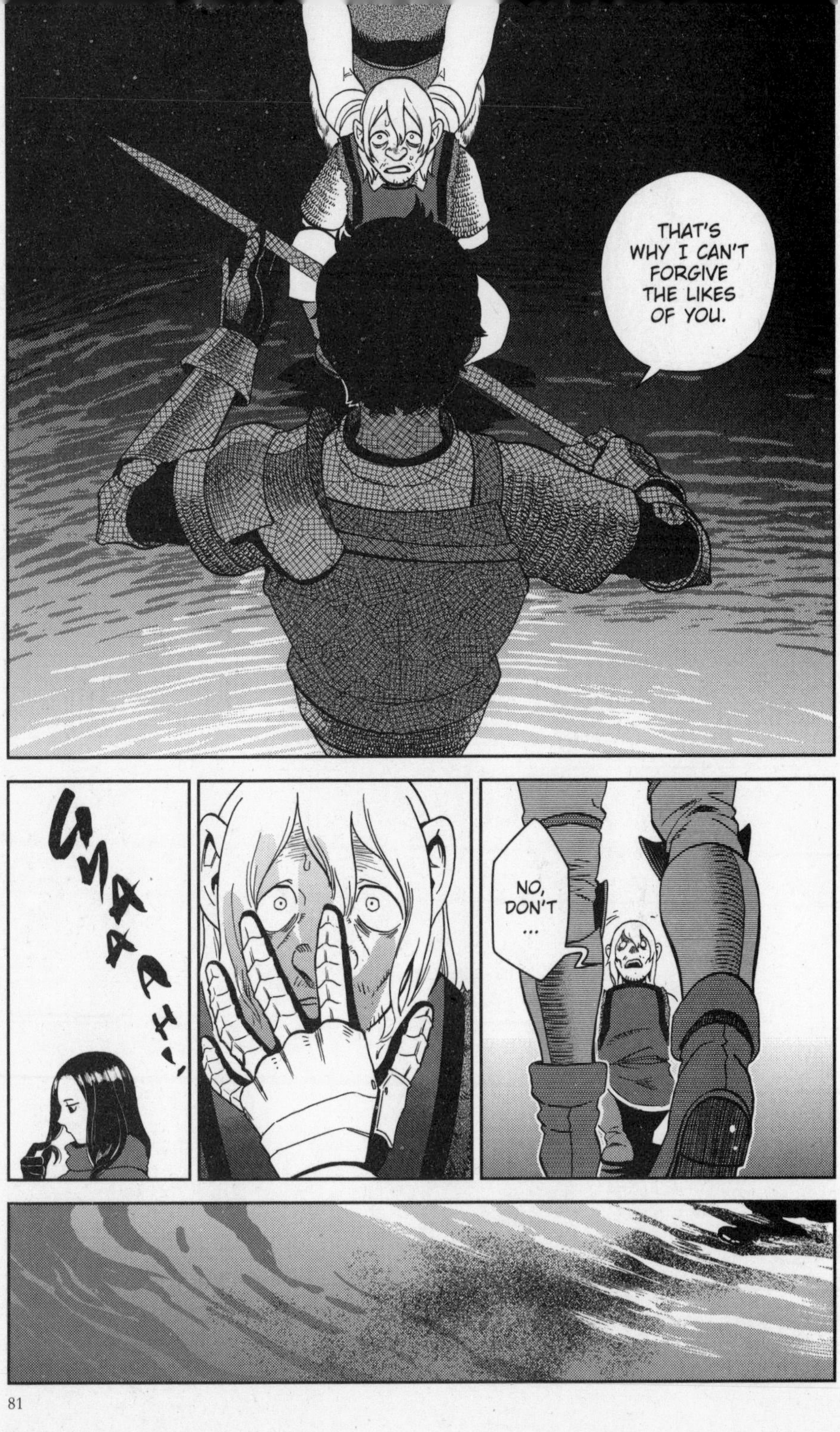

THAT'S WHY I CAN'T FORGIVE THE LIKES OF YOU.

UWAAAH!

NO, DON'T ...

GESHI (KICK)
BOCHA (SPLASH)

POI (TOSS)

KABRU.
DOBON (SPLOOSH)

...HM?

OH. SORRY ABOUT EARLIER.
THAT'S ALL I COULD MANAGE THAT QUICKLY.

*RIN'S PERSPECTIVE

WHAT DO YOU MEAN?
I DON'T KNOW. OR CARE.
OKAY, IF YOU'RE SURE.

I JUST KEEP FEELING IMPATIENT...
...AND I CAN'T SEEM TO MAKE ANY PROGRESS.

TRUE. THIS IS WHERE THAT IMPATIENCE LANDED US.
THE LOWEST. THE WORST.
WOULD IT KILL YOU TO BE ENCOURAG-ING?

THERE'S NO SENSE SUGAR-COATING IT.
THIS IS THE BEST WE CAN DO NOW.

TO THE LORD OF THE ISLAND, THE DUNGEON IS JUST A PROFITABLE HOLE.
EVEN IF THE GOLD AND SILVER RUN OUT, HE THINKS HE CAN EKE OUT A LIVING ON MONSTER HIDES AND BONES.

NO ONE GOES DOWN INTO FULLY EXPLORED DUNGEONS, THOUGH.
MAYBE BECAUSE THEY CAN'T DREAM OF STRIKING IT RICH.
MAYBE BECAUSE IT DOESN'T EXCITE THEIR SPIRIT OF ADVENTURE.

THE POPULATION DROPS, THEN DROPS AGAIN.
MONSTERS FLOOD OUT OF THE DUNGEON AND TORMENT THE RESI-DENTS.

MANY VILLAGES FELL INTO RUIN THAT WAY.

WE HAVE TO BREAK THE DUN-GEON'S CURSE, FAST.
THIS WORLD DOESN'T NEED DUNGEONS OR MON-STERS.

MM-HM.

I'M HUNGRY.
...BEING REVIVED DOES MAKE YOU HUNGRY, DOESN'T IT?

KABRU! KABRU!
THOSE GUYS HAD LOTS OF VALUABLE STUFF!
GREAT.
TAKE THEIR FOOD, THEN THROW THE REST IN THE WATER.

HUH!? SINK IT!?
IF WE TOOK THAT, WE'D BE JUST LIKE THEM...

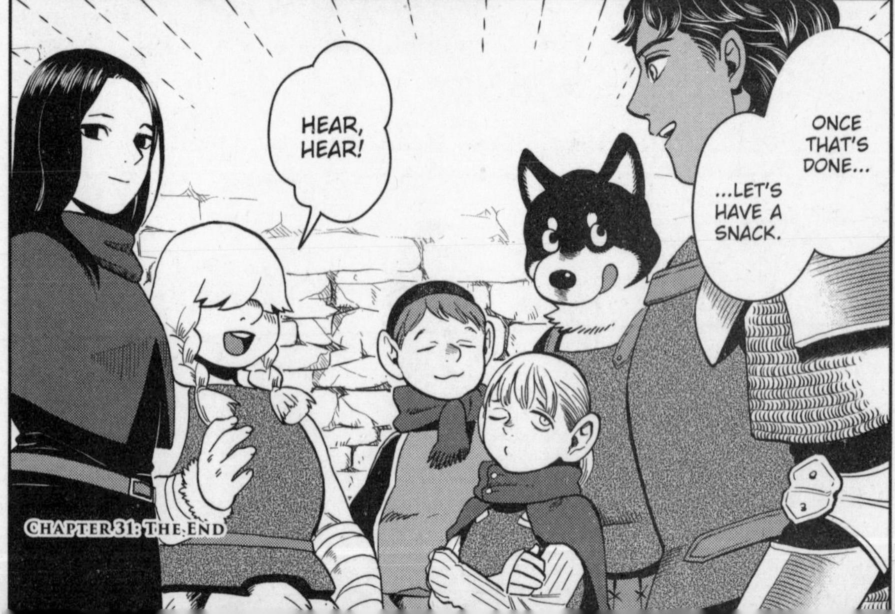

ONCE THAT'S DONE...
...LET'S HAVE A SNACK.
HEAR, HEAR!

CHAPTER 31: THE END

32. Sea Serpent, Part 2

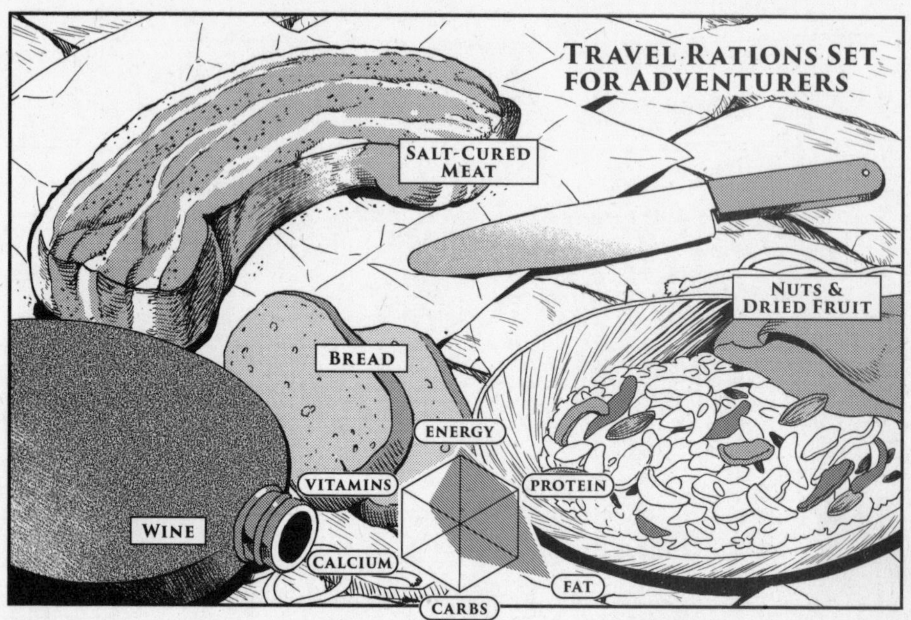
Travel Rations Set for Adventurers
Salt-Cured Meat
Nuts & Dried Fruit
Bread
Energy
Vitamins
Protein
Wine
Calcium
Fat
Carbs

THANKS FOR THE FOOD!

ぱくん
PAKUN (CHOMP)
もぐ…
MOGU (CHEW)
YUM!
THEY WERE EATING GOOD STUFF.
CORPSE RETRIEVAL PAYS WELL, DOESN'T IT?
SURE, IF YOU MAKE YOUR OWN CORPSES.

THE LORD OF THE ISLAND HASN'T CAUGHT ON?
I HEAR THERE'S SOME SORT OF REVIEW REGARDING REWARDS FROM THE ISLAND...
...BUT I GUESS THEY WERE PRETTY CLEVER ABOUT IT.
EITHER THAT, OR THEY WERE WORKING WITH LOTS OF OTHER PARTIES.
CORRUPTION...
むぐ
MUGU (MUNCH)
むぐ
MUGU
THEY'RE JUST DIGGING THEIR OWN GRAVES.

ARE WE REPORTING THIS TO THE LORD?
I DOUBT HE'D COME UP WITH GOOD COUNTER-MEASURES.
BEGINNERS LIKE DONI WOULD JUST END UP PAYING FOR IT.
DONI
YOU THINK THAT IDIOT LORD WILL KEEP GETTING FATTER AND BURST?
IF HE DOES, THE ELVES WILL SWOOP IN BEFORE YOU CAN BLINK.
WE NEED HIM TO HANG IN THERE AS A BULWARK FOR NOW.

STILL, A TALL-MAN, A DWARF...
...A HALF-FOOT, AND AN ELF, HM...?

WHAT ARE YOU TALKING ABOUT?
KUCHA (SNARF) KUCHA
THE PARTY THAT PUT THE GHOST WARD ON US.

OH. THE JEWEL THIEVES.
THE FOOD STEAL-ERS.

THERE AREN'T MANY PARTIES WITH ELVES IN THEM.
IF WE NARROW THE FIELD A BIT, WE MAY BE ABLE TO IDENTIFY THEM.

NO! IT WASN'T FIONIL, WAS IT!?
AH!
I DOUBT DONI'S GROUP WOULD BE DOWN ON THE THIRD FLOOR.
FIONIL

THAT "PARTY OF FOUR" BIT BOTHERS ME TOO.
PLUS, ONE OF THOSE FOUR IS A HALF-FOOT.
THAT'S A RECKLESS WAY TO EXPLORE.

RIN. HOLM.
DOES THIS GHOST WARD TELL YOU ANYTHING?

YOU'RE STILL WEARING THAT!?
IT'S TECH-NICALLY EVIDENCE.

I DON'T KNOW MUCH ABOUT THAT SORT OF MAGIC.
PAKU (CHOMP) ぱく
...LET ME SEE.

..."HONOR STUDENT."
PE (TOSS)
IT FEELS LIKE SHE DID IT BY THE BOOK.
AND IT'S NOT A SPELL SHE DOES OFTEN.

SHE MAY BE A MAGIC SCHOOL GRADUATE.
THOSE PEOPLE ALL WRITE SIMILAR FORMU-LAS.

IT DEFINITELY WAS AN ELF WHO WROTE IT...
...

SOWA (FIDGET) そわ...
MAGIC... SCHOOL ...

HMM.
MAGIC SCHOOL...
SOWA そわ
SOWA そわ
SOWA そわ
I SEE...

WHAT? WHAT IS IT?
WELL...
...I JUST HAD A THOUGHT.

IT'S ONLY A GUESS, BUT...
STILL...
WOW, I HOPE I'M RIGHT.
WHAT? DON'T BE A SMART-ASS.

UM...
THE TOUDEN SIBLINGS' PARTY.

*THE* TOU-DENS?
THEY DON'T SEEM THE TYPE WHO'D TURN TO CRIME.
WHY THEM?

FIRST!
THE TOUDEN SISTER GRADUATED FROM MAGIC SCHOOL!
......

BUT THE GHOST WARD WAS CAST BY AN ELF, RIGHT?
THE SIBLINGS ARE TALL-MEN.

HANG ON.
JUST HEAR ME OUT.

THE ELF IN THEIR PARTY SEEMED REALLY CLOSE TO THE SISTER.
AS IF THEY'D BEEN FRIENDS SINCE THEY WERE SMALL.
YOU CUT THEM YOURSELF AGAIN!?
SO... I THOUGHT MAYBE THEY'D GONE TO THE SAME MAGIC SCHOOL.

MAGIC SCHOOL GRADUATES ARE RARE AROUND HERE.
ESPE-CIALLY ELVES.

HM. I GUESS IT'S POSSIBLE, BUT...
THAT'S NOT SOLID PROOF.

IN ANY CASE, THERE WAS ONLY ONE TALL-MAN SCENT.
IF IT WERE THE SIBLINGS, THERE'D BE TWO...

...OH.

DON'T TELL ME...
THAT'S WHY THEY'RE GOING IN RECKLESSLY WITH SUCH A SMALL GROUP!?
EXACTLY!

THEY LOST EITHER THE BROTHER OR THE SISTER ...
...AND THEN FOUGHT ABOUT WHETHER TO GO RESCUE THEM.

I THINK SO...
...BECAUSE WE JUST PASSED ONE OF THEM.
WHAT?

THEY'VE BEEN ARGUING ABOUT GOALS AND REVENUE FOR A WHILE.
THAT PUT THEM IN A BIND, SO THEY TOOK OUR JEWELS AND FOOD...

SEVERAL OF THEIR PARTY MAY HAVE LEFT OVER THIS.

THIS IS STARTING TO SOUND PLAUSIBLE.
ISN'T IT!?

HM? BUT YOU SAID YOU SMELLED A DWARF TOO, KURO.
I DID.
IT REALLY SMELLED.
KUN KUN (SNIFF)

ISN'T THAT WEIRD, THEN?
THEY STILL HAVE A DWARF.
THEY MIGHT HAVE HIRED A NEW ONE.

WHO ELSE IS IN THAT PARTY?
LET'S SEE.
THE TALLMEN ARE LAIOS AND FALIN.
THEN THERE'S SHURO, WHO'S PROBABLY AN EASTERNER.
NAMARI, THE DWARF WE JUST SAW.
MARCILLE THE ELF.
THE HALF-FOOT IS "CHILCHUCK," OR SOMETHING LIKE THAT.

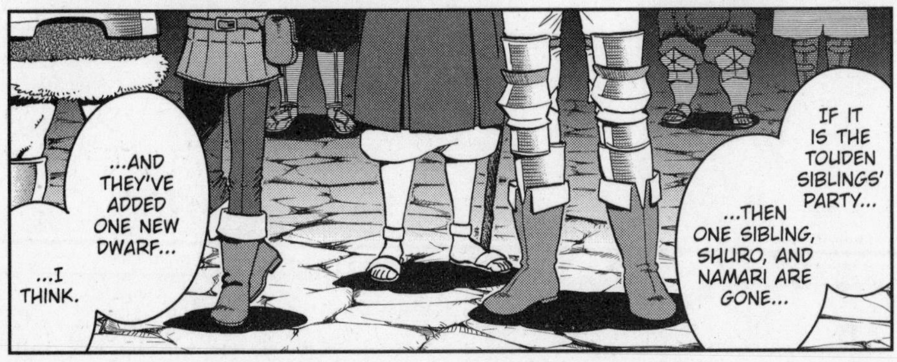

IF IT IS THE TOUDEN SIBLINGS' PARTY...
...THEN ONE SIBLING, SHURO, AND NAMARI ARE GONE...
...AND THEY'VE ADDED ONE NEW DWARF...
...I THINK.

I SEE. SO THAT WAS NAMARI.
HM.
DO YOU KNOW SOMETHING, DAYA?

JUST THE NAME. SHE'S FAMOUS.
THE ONLY DAUGHTER OF A MAN THEY CALL "THE WEAPONS DEALER."

THE WEAPONS DEALER?
HE USED TO MANAGE THE ISLAND'S WEAPONS DISTRIBU-TION.

BUT ONE DAY, THEY FOUND THAT LARGE SUMS HAD BEEN EMBEZZLED, AND HE DIS-APPEARED.
THEY SAY IT'S ONE OF THE THINGS THAT SOURED THE ISLAND LORD'S PERCEPTION OF DWARFS.

LOTS OF DWARFS HAD A HARD TIME BECAUSE OF THAT...
ME TOO.
I DOUBT ANY DECENT DWARF WOULD TAKE HER SPOT IN THE PARTY.

SO MAYBE IT'S NOT A DECENT DWARF.
IT SMELLED LIKE BAD NEWS.
ぼふっ
BOFU (WHUMP)

I KNOW ABOUT THAT CHILCHUCK GUY TOO.
HE'S AN OLD GEEZER.
HE ACTS LIKE HE'S THE REP FOR ALL THE ISLAND'S HALF-FOOTS.

HE'S LIKE, "WHEN YOU MAKE CONTRACTS, GO THROUGH THE GUILD.
"AND THEN PAY ME A BROKER'S FEE."
MONEY
MONEY
MONEY
HE'S A GREEDY JERK!

I TOLD HIM I'M NOT JOINING ANY SUCH THING AND RAN OFF.
I MEAN, IF THEY KNEW I'D HIRED A KOBOLD, THEY'D COME TO "HAVE A TALK" WITH ME.

YOU'D HATE THAT, RIGHT?
YOU WANT TO WORK FOR ME, RIGHT, KURO?
MIK GIVES ME FOOD.
SHE'S A GOOD BOSS!

YOU'RE SO RIGHT!
なでこ NADEKO
なでこ NADEKO (PET)
IF I HADN'T TAKEN YOU IN, YOU'D BE OUT ON THE STREETS RIGHT NOW!

...I BET KURO'S BEING WORKED LIKE A DOG FOR PEANUTS.
HOLM.
YOU SHOULDN'T SAY THINGS LIKE THAT BASED ON SPECULA-TION.
EE HEE HEE!

SO THAT EASTERN TALL-MAN...
HE'S FROM YOUR AREA, RIGHT, RIN?
DO YOU KNOW HIM?
LISTEN...
...DON'T LUMP ALL EASTERNERS TOGETHER.

SOME PLACES DON'T EVEN SPEAK THE SAME LANGUAGE.
AND BESIDES, I WAS BORN HERE.
"SHURO" ISN'T A NAME FROM MY ISLAND.

—IN THAT CASE, I MAY KNOW MORE THAN YOU.

HE WAS A STANDOUT THERE TOO.
HE CAME TO THE ISLAND WITH A FEW FRIENDS FROM HOME...
...THEN JOINED THE TOUDEN PARTY BY HIMSELF.

HE SEEMED PRETTY SHADY.
HE TOOK ON THE DUNGEON TO TEST HIS SKILLS.

SO HE LEFT THE PARTY, HUH?
HE DIDN'T LOOK LIKE HE'D CARE ABOUT REWARDS OR DANGER...

DID THEY LOSE BOTH THE SIBLINGS, AND HE STAYED?
ブツ BUTSU (MUTTER)
ブツ BUTSU
...NO, PROBABLY NOT.

KABRU, YOU REMEMBER SO MUCH ABOUT OTHER PEOPLE THAT IT'S CREEPY.
IT'S A HOBBY.

WHY DO YOU LOOK LIKE YOU'RE ENJOYING THIS?

PA (BEAM)
BECAUSE I AM!
THIS IS LOTS OF FUN!

THERE ARE TONS OF PEOPLE ON THIS ISLAND...
...AND THEY'RE ALL ACTING FOR THEIR OWN REA-SONS.

BUT WHEN ALL THOSE SEPARATE ACTIONS ...
...ARE MESHED TOGETH-ER...

...IT BECOMES A HISTORIC EVENT INVOLVING LOTS AND LOTS OF PEOPLE.

I THOUGHT THIS WAS A BORING CASE OF THEFT...
...BUT I'VE GOT A HUNCH THAT SOMETHING INTERESTING'S GOING TO HAPPEN.

I REALLY HOPE IT'S THE TOUDEN SIBLINGS' PARTY.
SOWA (FIDGET)
SOWA
AFTER ALL...

...I'VE BEEN WAITING FOR AGES...

...FOR SOMEBODY TO UNMASK THEM.

YOU'VE GOT A BONE TO PICK WITH THEM?
AAAH.
THEY DIDN'T DO ANYTHING TO ME.

LONG AGO, I HEAR THEY WORKED IN A BAND OF GOLD-PEELERS.
THEY GAVE MOST OF THEIR EARNINGS TO SICK OR INJURED COMPANIONS WHO COULDN'T GO INTO THE DUNGEON ANYMORE.

HUH.
BORI (MUNCH) BORI
SOUNDS GOOD TO ME.

YES. IT'S AN ADMIRABLE STORY.
BUT THERE'S MORE TO IT.

THEIR COMPANIONS HAD HEALED UP AGES AGO, BUT THEY TOOK THE MONEY ANYWAY.
IN THE END, THEY NEVER WENT BACK TO ADVEN-TURING.
NOW, THEY SELL ILLEGALLY MANU-FACTURED GOODS ON THE ISLAND.

"THE ONE TO DEFEAT THE LORD OF THE DUNGEON WILL BE GIVEN EVERY-THING."
THEY SAY THE MAN WHO WAS KING OF THIS COUNTRY SAID SO.
HOWEVER, EVEN IF YOU AREN'T REALLY GIVEN EVERY-THING...
...THE DUNGEON ITSELF IS A RELIC OF THE ANCIENT ELVES.
THERE'S NO DOUBT THAT YOU'D GAIN GREAT INFLUENCE.
AND SO...

...I DON'T THINK IT SHOULD BE THOSE SIBLINGS.
IT'S NOT THAT THEY'RE BAD PEOPLE.
THEY JUST AREN'T INTER-ESTED IN HUMANS.
JUST LIKE THE ISLAND'S LORD.

AND TO OUST THAT STUPID LORD OF THE ISLAND TOO.

WE KNOW, KABRU.
WE THINK YOU'RE THE ONLY ONE WHO'S FIT TO LEAD.

IF WE REPORTED THE THEFT, COULDN'T WE RUN THOSE MEN OFF THE ISLAND?
WE'D HAVE TO STAKE OUT THE TOWN AND CATCH THEM WITH THE GOODS.

WELL, IF WE'RE STILL HAVING TROUBLE WITH RANDOM MONSTERS, WE'VE STILL GOT A LONG WAY TO GO.
YOU'RE RIGHT.

チャプ
CHAPU (PLISH)

SHALL WE GO, THEN?
LET'S HOPE WE GET BACK WITHOUT TROUBLE.

AGH!
PASHA (SPLASH)

LOOK OUT!
PA (FWP)
PA
BLADE FISH!
PA
PA
......
PA

AH!
DON'T LET THEM DISTRACT YOU!
WATCH WHAT'S UNDER YOUR FEET—

もぉ…
GUMOO (SWELL)

A KRA—
NO, A SEA SERPENT!!
ZA (SPLSH)
ZA
RIN!
GET BA—
DON (BOOM)
MMPH!

BOYON (BOING)
ボヨン
……
……

CHANT...

RGH...

BUORUN
ブォル
BORURURURUN
ボルルルルン
I CAN'T BRING "HER" OUT WHEN IT'S LIKE THIS!
WEIRD STUFF WOULD GET MIXED IN.
BUORUN (BLORP)

... HOLM!
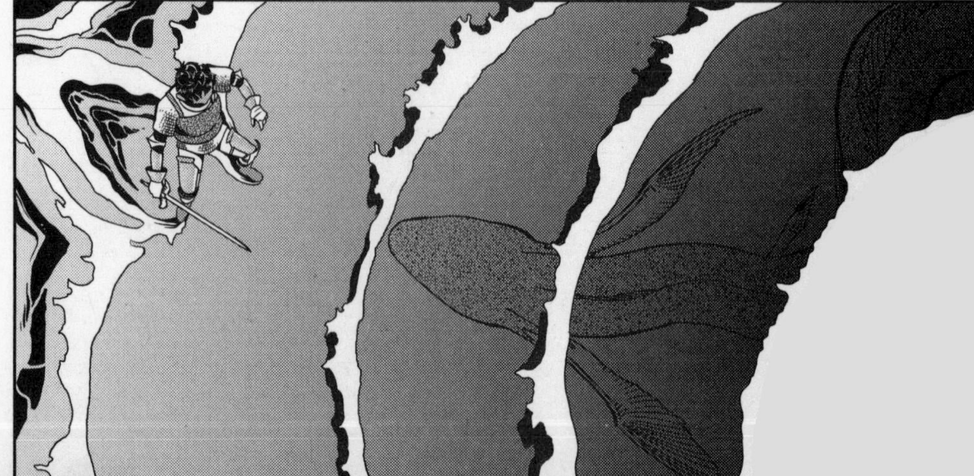

DON'T PANIC.
YOU HAVE TO HANDLE IT, KABRU.
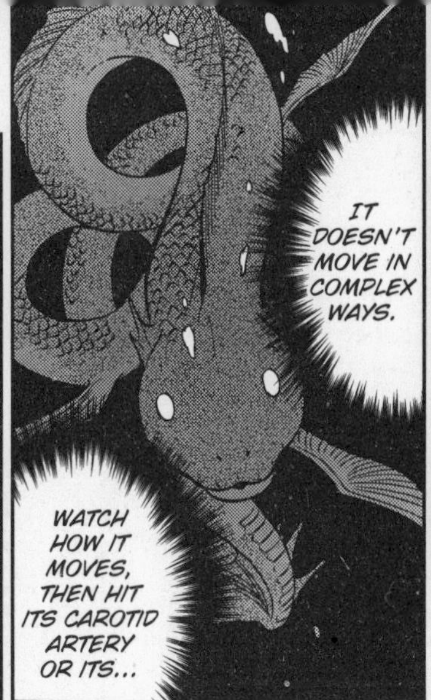
IT DOESN'T MOVE IN COMPLEX WAYS.
WATCH HOW IT MOVES, THEN HIT ITS CAROTID ARTERY OR ITS...

WAIT. WHERE IS ITS CAROTID ARTERY?
TON (TMP)
'SCUSE ME.

SHU
(WHIP)
PAAAN
(BLAM)

TADE!
YUP-YUP!
GUU (TENSE)
DOGOO (WHUDD)

GURAAA (TEETER)
IT'S ALL YOURS, YOUNG MASTER!
GOOO (WHOOM)
OOO (WHOOSH)

つ…
TSU (SST)
チャン
CHIN (TING)
ドボ
DOBO (BLOOSH)
ドボン
DOBON

PASHA (SPLASH)
YOUNG MASTER!!

THAT WAS SPLENDID.
WERE YOUR CLOTHES SOILED?
PHEW...
NO.

YOU MUST BE TIRED.
WHY DON'T WE HAVE OUR MEAL HERE?
SOME TEA?
NO NEED.
WE'RE IN A HURRY.

SFX: GUUURURURU (GURGLE)

HE'S A TROUBLE-SOME MASTER.
HE'S COMPLETELY SMITTEN WITH THAT NORTHERN GIRL.
TADE'S SUPER-HUNGRY NOW.

WOULDN'T THIS BE YUMMY IF WE STEWED IT WITH RADISHES?
ARE YOU AN IDIOT?

KABRU? ARE YOU HURT?

CHANGE OF PLANS.
HUH?

EXCUSE ME.

THANK YOU FOR HELPING ME WHEN I WAS IN DANGER.
I'M KABRU.
MAY I ASK YOUR NAME?

MY...!

DON'T WORRY ABOUT IT.
I'M JUST PASSING THROUGH.

IF I'M NOT MISTAKEN ...
...ARE YOU SEARCHING FOR A WOMAN?

ばっ
BA (TURN)

D-DO YOU KNOW SOME-THING!?
AH. I WAS RIGHT.
YOU HAVE MY SYM-PATHY.

I MAY BE OF SOME ASSISTANCE ...
...IN YOUR SEARCH FOR MISS FALIN TOUDEN.
......!
GRRR
HEY! KURO! I TOLD YOU NOT TO MAKE THAT FACE.
IT'S SCARY.
RRR
RRRRRR...
HONESTLY! WHAT'S THE MATTER WITH IT?

# 33. Dryad

TWO FULL DAYS AFTER DECIDING TO RETURN TO THE SURFACE...
I DON'T WANT TO LOSE YOU.
YOU GUYS...
...LAIOS AND COMPANY WERE...

IT'S A DEAD END.
ANOTHER DEAD END.
......

...LOST, AND NEAR DEATH.
I'M HUNGRY...
I'M SLEEPY...
I'M THIRSTY...

ZU
ズ
ZU
ズ
ZU (RUMBLE)
ズズ
WHOA!
ZU
ズズ
ZU
ズズ
ANOTHER EARTH-QUAKE?

DAMN IT! WHAT GIVES !?
DAN (SLAM)
ダン!
THIS WALL WAS NOT HERE LAST TIME WE CAME THROUGH.

IT'S NOT AN EARTH-QUAKE.
THE DUNGEON IS MOVING, CHANGING ITS SHAPE.

I BET IT'S THE MAGICIAN'S DOING.
SHE MAY BE ON HER GUARD AGAINST US.

YOU MEAN SHE'S MAKING US WANDER IN CIRCLES FOREVER?
SOWA (FIDGET)
SOWA
LET'S TRY MIXING IT UP, THEN.

HANG ON A SECOND.
HUP!

PATATA (FLUTTER)
パタタ...

BASA (FLAP)

I THINK IT'S GONE.
BERI (PEEL)

......

STILL, SOMEHOW, THE TOWN SEEMS TO BE...

GOING OVER THE WALL MAY NOT BE WISE.
SO WE SHOULD KEEP LOOKING FOR A PATH?

TA (TAP)
TA
TA
TON (CLACK)
TOOON

KUH
KUH

HYEH
HYEH
HEH

...SLOWLY GETTING LIVELIER.
THE RED DRAGON'S DEAD, SO THE MONSTERS THAT WERE HIDING HAVE COME OUT.

THIS LEVEL ALWAYS HAD LOTS OF MONSTERS.
NOT MEETING THEM EARLIER WAS SHEER GOOD LU—

ZUKI (PANG)
GH...

DO (WHUD)
MUGYU (SQUISH)
H-HEY!

HMM.

WE'VE BEEN WALKING EVER SINCE WE LEFT THE ORCS.
WE HAVEN'T HAD A DECENT MEAL SINCE WE ATE THE DRAGON.

THIS ISN'T HEALTHY.

I CAN'T REALLY TELL LAIOS'S AGE...
IS HE YOUNG OR FULL-GROWN?
...BUT CHILCHUCK AND MARCILLE ARE PROBABLY STILL GROWING.
THIS IS GOOD.

AT SUCH AN AGE, AND I CAN'T FEED THEM PROPERLY.
THE SHAME IS OVER-WHELMING.

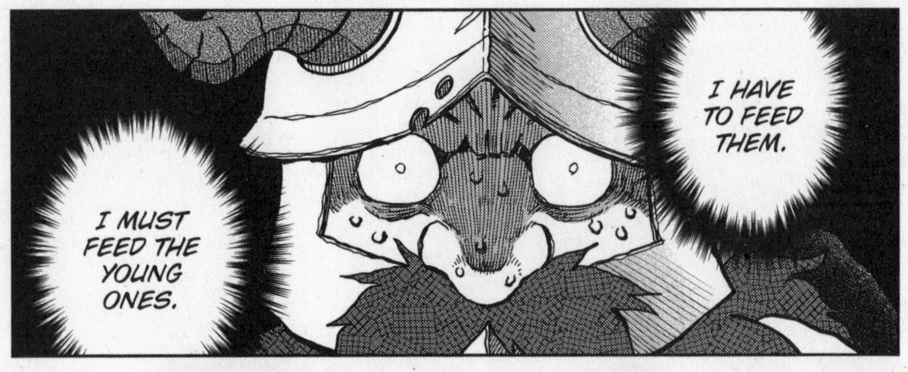
I HAVE TO FEED THEM.
I MUST FEED THE YOUNG ONES.

THE ORCS SHARED SOME RE-SOURCES WITH US...
...BUT LOSING THAT PRESERVED DRAGON MEAT HURT.

HM?
HIKU (TWITCH)
I SMELL...

...SOME-THING SWEET.
KUN (SNIFF)
KUN
IS IT FOOD?

NO. MORE LIKE FLOWERS.
!

WHERE FLOWERS BLOOM, THERE'S WATER...
FIND IT, CHIL!
I'M ON IT!

くんくん
KUN (SNIFF)
KUN
くん
KUN
ガサッ
GASA (RUSTLE)

THIS PLACE...
IS IT A GRAVE-YARD OR SOME-THING?

HAH...
WAIT. SOME-BODY'S HERE.

DON'T LOOK !!
BA (GRAB)
AH!?

HEH!
HEH!

HEE HEE!

W-WE BEG YOUR PARDON...
HEY, SENSHI, LET GO—

BA (FWOOM)
WHOA !?

TCH!
GET BACK, SENSHI !!
DON (SHUNK)
BA
BECHA (SPLAT)
MMPF!
WHAT WAS THAT!?
PTOO!
PTOO!
DRAW YOUR WEAP-ON!
THEY'RE NOT HUMAN!
KOFF!
THEY'RE DRYAD FLOW-ERS!

THEN THIS FLUID IS...
IT'S NOT A LIQUID.
THESE ULTRA-FINE PARTICLES ENTER THE RESPIRATORY SYSTEM...
...THEN CLING TO THE MUCUS MEMBRANES.
THE BODY RECOGNIZES THESE PARTICLES, LABELS THEM "HARMFUL"...
...MOBILIZES ITS IMMUNE SYSTEM, AND SWIFTLY ACTS TO EXPEL THEM.

MUZU (ITCH) MUZU

BORO BORO (DRIP)

BURU (SHIVER) BURU
BUH...
??
BUH...

IT'S WHAT THEY CALL "HAY FEVER."
BWAAACHOO!

DWEE-CHOO!
BWAAA-CHOO!
WHOA! WHAT!? GROSS!
ACHOO!
AH! OW!

DRYAD POLLEN, HUH!?
YACHOO
WACHOO
OWW...
GURU (WRAP)
NOT GOOD. DON'T BREATHE IT, SENSHI.

HEY, HEY! THIS IS BAD.
THE TEARS WON'T STOP.

MY WHOLE BODY ITCHES SO MUCH IT BURNS.
BARI
BARI (SCRATCH)

HAAAGK...
HAA...
I CAN'T BREATHE ...

SHA (FWISH)
WAUGH!
DON (BAM)
GET UP AND SNAP OUT OF IT, SENSHI.
BWEH.
LAIOS!
KENSUKE...
KENSUKE...
DAMN IT.
HFF!
HFF!
MY EYES ARE GETTING...
HFF!

...SENSHI.
STRETCH OUT YOUR HAND.
ON MY SIGNAL, SLASH BEHIND YOU WITH IT.

GIRI
ONE...
GIRI
TWO, AND...
GIRI (KRNCH)

THREE!!
BASA (FWISH)
BA (FOOM)
HNRGH!

ZU (SHUNK)

GHK ...!

ZU (GRIT)

BUN (SWIPE)

HIRARI (FLIT)

ヒュ
HYU (ZWIP)
ヒュ
HYU
ド
DO
ド
DO (THUD)
ヒュ
HYU
ド
DO
SENSHI, RUN FOR IT!
I CAN'T!
I HAVE TO PROTECT THE YOUNG PEOPLE.
WHAT'S THAT SUP-POSED TO...
YOU BE MY EYES, CHIL-CHUCK.
I CAN'T. I CAN'T SEE A THING.
ALL YOUR SENSES ARE SHARP, AREN'T THEY?
......
ズビ
ZUBI (SNIFF)

SMELL...
IT'S NO GOOD. THE SCENT OF THE POLLEN IS TOO STRONG.

BWACHOO
AND SOUND... SENSHI'S SNEEZES ARE NOISY!!
I CAN'T TRUST MY EYES, NOSE, OR EARS...

FU (FWSH)

WIND!

IT AVOIDED YOUR SNEEZE AND DODGED BEHIND YOU TO THE RIGHT!
SWING UP JUST LIKE THAT, SENSHI!

ZAN
(SKASH)

SNAPPED RIGHT IN TWO...
HAAAAH...
IF I DON'T FIX IT AND GIVE IT MANA QUICKLY, THE STAFF WILL DIE.

SURI (STROKE)
AND AFTER IT TOOK YEARS TO GROW IT THIS MUCH...
GASA (RUSTLE) GASA GASA

DOROO (OOZE)
AAAAAAH!

IT...
BURU BURU BURU (SHAKE)
IT...

IT'S SAFE IN HERE...
BOTA BOTA BOTA (DRIP)
LIAR!!

YOU WERE FIGHTING DRYAD FLOWERS?
THAT MUST HAVE BEEN ROUGH.
BASHA (SPLASH)
バシャ

STILL, FLOWER MON-STERS...
I WAS SURE THEY WERE REAL MEN AND WOMEN.

DRYADS ARE DIOECIOUS FLOWERS, SO "MALE" AND "FEMALE" IS RIGHT...
OH.
I WONDER IF...

GASA (RUSTLE)
ガサ
GASA
ガサ
ガサ
GASA

WHAT SHOULD WE DO?
SHOULDN'T WE HIT HIM AND MAKE HIM STOP?
HE'S LOOKING FOR SOMETHING...

...WE CAN'T BE PICKY NOW. IT FEELS LIKE...
..."AT THIS POINT, SO WHAT IF THE FLOWERS LOOK HUMAN?"

MARCI—
AAAH!!

I FOUND SOME!!

TURN BACK...
...TIME...
NO, QUIT IT!!
DON'T JUST START LOOKING FOR RISKY-SOUNDING SPELLS!
THAT CAN'T BE IN THERE!!

YOUR BLACK MAGIC JOKES AREN'T FUNNY!

NO POLLEN CAME OUT OF THE LAST DRYAD I CUT.

IT WAS PROBABLY A FEMALE.
BEFORE THEY'RE POLLINATED, FLOWERS CARE FOR AND PROTECT THE FRUIT.

......

THIS LOOKS LIKE FRUIT TOO.
OH, THAT'S A BUD.
WHEN IT GETS BIGGER, IT WILL TURN INTO A DRYAD FLOWER.

THESE LOOK EASIER TO EAT.
SO THESE ARE FINE...? WEIRD.
THEY MIGHT BE PRETTY GOOD.
LET'S PICK THEM.
PUCHI (SNAP)

SU (SHF)

...DON'T TAKE TOO MANY.

...ALL RIGHT.

HEY.
MAN-DRAKES.

THERE'S NO TIME TO GET A DOG, SO I'LL JUST CUT OFF ITS HEAD, OKAY?
OH, SHUT UP.
JUST DROP IT, WOULD YOU!?

ARE THESE EDIBLE?
LET ME SEE.

HM.
THAT'S A PRETTY GOOD HARVEST.

BORROWING AN AX FROM THE ORCS WAS A GOOD IDEA.
I ALMOST TOOK A SPEAR...
?

ばっ
BAKAN (WHUNK)

ドキ ドキ
DOKI (BADMP) DOKI
GOOD, VERY GOOD.

PUT THE CHOPPED INGREDIENTS IN A POT WITH WATER AND BOIL THEM.
FUTSU (BUBBLE)
FUTSU

WHEN THEY'RE SOFT, TAKE THEM OFF THE HEAT...
...AND MASH THEM IN THE POT.

ONCE YOU HAVE A PASTE, ADD MORE WATER, THEN SEASON IT.

HMM...

SHAKU (SLICE)

MM. IT SMELLS GOOD.
IN THAT CASE...

SAUTE LIGHTLY IN BUTTER.

ADD MUSHROOMS.

POUR MELTED CHEESE OVER THE TOP, AND...
TOROO (DRIZZLE)

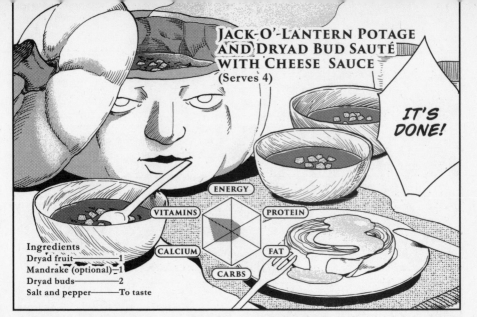

## Jack-O'-Lantern Potage and Dryad Bud Sauté with Cheese Sauce

(Serves 4)

IT'S DONE!

ENERGY
PROTEIN
FAT
CARBS
CALCIUM
VITAMINS

Ingredients

| | |
|---|---|
| Dryad fruit | 1 |
| Mandrake (optional) | 1 |
| Dryad buds | 2 |
| Salt and pepper | To taste |

WHY DID YOU PUT IT IN THAT?
I THOUGHT IT MIGHT HELP REPLENISH YOUR MANA A BIT MORE.

HIDING BEHIND GOOD INTEN-TIONS DOESN'T MAKE IT OKAY!
I'LL EAT IT, BUT...

WOW! IT'S SWEET. THERE'S A FAINT FLORAL FRAGRANCE TO IT.
IT'S REALLY RICH, BUT IT MELTS IN YOUR MOUTH...


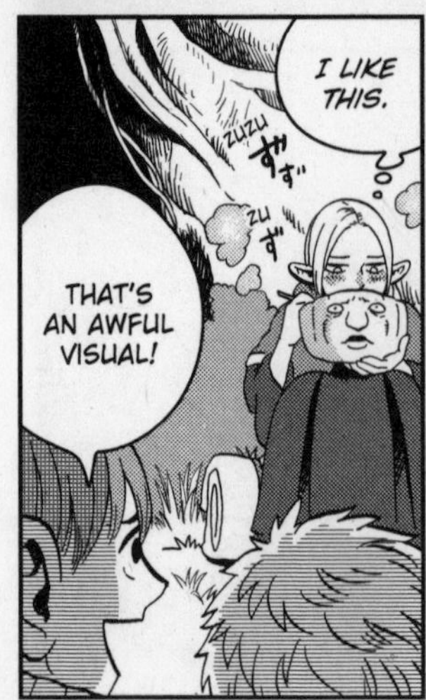

I LIKE THIS.
ZUZU
ずず
ZU
ず
THAT'S AN AWFUL VISUAL!

キコキコ
KIKO (SAW) KIKO

トローリ
TORORI (DRIBBLE)

THE CHEESE'S ACIDITY WORKS WELL HERE.
I LIKED THE SLIGHT BITTER-NESS IT HAD.

SO HOW ARE WE GOING TO GET OUT?
WHAT IF WE'RE STUCK IN HERE FOREVER?

SEALING ALL THE PATHS TO THE SURFACE ...
...WOULD CUT OFF THE FLOW OF MANA, SO I DOUBT SHE WILL.

THERE MUST BE A WAY OUT SOME-WHERE.
パク
PAKU (CHOMP)

IS THERE ANY LOGIC TO THE CHANGES IN THE DUNGEON?
THAT'S IT!
LET'S JOT DOWN MAPS AND THE INTERVALS BETWEEN TREMORS.

I'M STARTING TO THINK THIS MIGHT WORK OUT.
...
THINGS LOOK BETTER ON A FULL STOMACH.

AAAH...
PWAH!
I'M ALL WARM NOW.

I THINK I MAY HAVE RECOVERED SOME MANA.
WE HAVE TO TREAT YOUR WOUNDS, LAIOS AND SENSHI.

YOU SHOULDN'T PUSH YOURSELF YET...
I'M NOT GOING TO.

LAIOS!
PI (POINT)
YOU HAVE TO STEP UP.

I'LL TEACH YOU MAGIC.

I CAN'T PROTECT ALL OF YOU FROM THE LUNATIC MAGICIAN BY MYSELF.
IF YOU LEARN HEALING AND DEFENSE SPELLS, IT'LL BE MUCH EASIER.

FALIN TAUGHT YOU THE BASICS, DIDN'T SHE?
TECHNI-CALLY...

SHE SPECIALIZES IN THE GNOME MAGIC SYSTEM.
IT'S A BIT DIFFERENT FROM THE SYSTEM I USE, BUT...
WELL, AT HEART, THEY'RE SIMILAR.
IT'S FINE. I'LL DRUM IT INTO YOU SOON ENOUGH.

WE HAVE TO GET STRONGER.

......!
RIGHT!

THIS GOES LIKE THIS, AND LIKE THAT...

THEY'RE TOO OPTI-MISTIC.
THAT'S HOW YOUNG PEOPLE SHOULD BE.

SATISFIED...
......

LOOK, WOULD YOU STOP TREATING ME LIKE A KID!?
I CAN'T TAKE IT!
AND WHY DID YOU COVER MY EYES WHEN THERE WERE MONSTERS AROUND!?
I MEAN, IT ENDED UP SAVING ME, BUT...

I SEE.
CHIL-CHUCK.

YOU SAID YOUR FATHER HAS PASSED, DIDN'T YOU?
YES. SO WHAT?
I SEE...

THIS IS A GOOD OPPORTUNITY. I'LL TEACH YOU.
?
YOU SIT THERE.

AT YOUR AGE, I BET THESE THINGS ARE STARTING TO INTEREST YOU...
...BUT YOU NEED TO HAVE PROPER KNOWLEDGE OF THEM.
ポキ
POKI (SNAP)
MEAN-
ING...?

RIGHT.
HUMANS ALSO HAVE STAMENS AND PISTILS...

AND SO IT WENT ...
...FAR INTO THE NIGHT.
W-R-O-N-G!!
LISTEN SERIOUSLY!!
CHAPTER 33: THE END

# 34. Cockatrice

GO ON. HURRY!
UM...
ちょん
CHON (TAP)
ふに…
FUNI (SQUISH)
ギュ
ム
GYUMU (SQUEEZE)

RUDE !!!
BASHI! (FLAP)
AGH!
I THOUGHT IT WOULD BE BAD TO TOUCH IT IN A WEIRD WAY...
THAT'S NOT THE POINT HERE!
PUT OUT YOUR LEFT HAND.
BACHI (SMACK)
ばち
THERE.
SURI (STROKE)
THIS IS FINE.
NH...
GETTING EMBAR-RASSED WON'T IMPROVE YOUR MAGIC!
COME ON, FOCUS! FOCUS!
SHE'S STRICT ...

BE AWARE OF THE MANA CIRCULATING INSIDE US.

VISUALIZE IT AS BLOOD VESSELS.

LINK THE FLOW THROUGH YOUR PALM...

...FROM THE TOP OF YOUR HEAD...

...TO THE TIPS OF MY TOES.

SYNCHRONIZE OUR BREATHING...
...TEMPERATURE, AND PULSE RATE...
WHEN YOU THINK YOU HAVE THE RHYTHM...
...CHANT AFTER ME.

GATTAAAN (CLATTER)
ITCHY!!!
A-ARE YOU OKAY!?
UUUURGH, IT ITCHES! IT ITCHES!
BORI BORI BORI (SCRATCH)
OH.
THE SCAB CAME OFF.
HUH!?
IT WORKED! YOU DID IT, LAIOS!
THAT'S AMAZING!
ARE YOU SURE?
YOU'RE BLEED-ING.
IT'S ALWAYS LIKE THIS AT FIRST.
YES, BECAUSE THE SCAB CAME OFF.
THE WAY YOU TAUGHT ME WAS NICE AND EASY TO UNDER-STAND.
THANKS.
YOU'RE A FAST LEARNER, THOUGH.
APTITUDE FOR THIS MUST RUN IN YOUR FAMILY!
I COULDN'T REALLY UNDERSTAND WHAT FALIN SAID.
THEN, WHEN IT FEELS RIGHT, YOU GO...
BWAH! AND THEN...
BA-BOOM!
SHE WORKS ON INSTINCT.

ALL RIGHT, BEFORE YOU FORGET HOW IT FEELS, TRY DOING IT TO SENSHI.

I'LL BE WATCHING.
DOKI DOKI (BADMP)
DOKI DOKI
JUST DO WHAT YOU DID BEFORE.

NOW THEN...
IT'S A STOPGAP, BUT...
...I'LL USE DRYAD TWIGS TO REPAIR IT.
KU (TUG) KU
I WONDER IF THEY'LL ASSIMILATE...

TSUU (WEAVE)

UM...

SO. (PAT)

BAD TOUCH ...
I-I'M SORRY...
I TOLD YOU, THAT'S NOT THE POINT!

COME ON, DON'T GET EMBARRASSED.
THIS IS AWKWARD...
EMBARRASSMENT IS IMPROVEMENT'S BIGGEST ENEMY.

...YOU REALLY CAN'T DISCOUNT THAT SORT OF STUFF.
HEALERS HAVE TO BE IN CONTACT WITH OTHERS A LOT, AND IT CREATES PROBLEMS.

HUMAN RELATIONSHIPS ARE WHAT BREAK UP MOST PARTIES.
ROMANCE, ENVY AND JEALOUSY, GRUDGES AND HATE...
IT'S A NUISANCE.

GRR.
HEY...

YOU'RE TALKING ABOUT FALIN AND SHURO, RIGHT?
IT'S JUST WHAT I'VE SEEN.

MORE THAN COMBAT SKILLS, LEADERS NEED THE ABILITY TO BIND PEOPLE TOGETHER.

FRANKLY, MORE THAN MAGIC...
...I'D RATHER LAIOS LEARNED HOW TO SOCIALIZE AND SIZE PEOPLE UP.
LIKE, SAY, KNOWING WHERE OTHER PEOPLE DON'T WANT TO BE TOUCHED.
IF HE HAD THAT...

...HE WOULDN'T HAVE GOTTEN ROPED INTO HELPING WITH BLACK MAGIC.

WHY DON'T YOU LEARN A BIT ABOUT MAGIC, CHILCHUCK?
AREN'T YOU JUST BLINDLY FEARFUL OF ITS REPUTATION?

OH, WOW, I'M SORRY ABOUT THAT!
ANY TIME A HALF-FOOT'S GOTTEN INVOLVED WITH ANTYHING TIED TO BLACK MAGIC..
...THEY'VE BEEN SNATCHED BY ELVES AND NEVER SEEN AGAIN...

...SO I NEVER HAD A CHANCE TO LEARN ABOUT IT IN DETAIL!
GEE, I'M SORRY I KNOW SO LITTLE.
......

THE ANCIENT MAGIC I'M RESEARCHING IS...
...PUT BRIEFLY ...

...MAGIC THAT DRAWS ENERGY...
...FROM ANOTHER DIMENSION WHERE "INFINITY" EXISTS.

ANOTHER DIMENSION...

HOW WOULD YOU TURN A CUPFUL OF WATER INTO VAPOR?
YOU'D PUT IT OVER A FIRE AND BOIL IT, RIGHT?
?

THEN WHAT ABOUT TURNING A WHOLE LAKE INTO VAPOR?
?
THE THEORY IS THE SAME...
...BUT ACTUALLY MAKING IT HAPPEN IS HARDER.

"COORDINATE MAGIC" SUPPORTS SPELLS THAT REQUIRE...
...VAST AMOUNTS OF POWER AND TIME.

IN MANY PLACES, THIS DUNGEON...
...IS LINKED TO ANOTHER DIMENSION.
THAT POWER IS USED TO SUMMON MONSTERS AND CREATE THE DUNGEON.

BACK THEN, FALIN NO LONGER HAD THE STRENGTH TO RECOVER ON HER OWN.

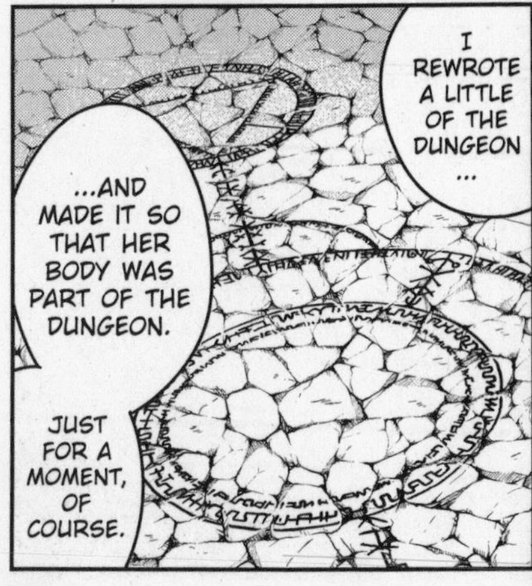
I REWROTE A LITTLE OF THE DUNGEON...
...AND MADE IT SO THAT HER BODY WAS PART OF THE DUNGEON.
JUST FOR A MOMENT, OF COURSE.

ZUN
(RUMBLE)

ANOTHER TREMOR.
ZUZU
ZU
ZU
IT'S CLOSE.

BA
(LUNGE)

LOOK OVER THERE.
THE WALL'S MOVING.

WHERE'S IT GOING?

WANT TO GO TAKE A LOOK?
SURE.

HUH?

GATA
(CLONK)
GATA
GATAAAN
(CLATTER)
GON
(WHUNK)

WH-WHAT'S WRONG!?
I GUH...
I GOT DIZZY ALL OF A...

...OH.
I BET HE HAS MANA SICKNESS.
HE DID JUST USE MANA FOR THE FIRST TIME.

IT SHOULD SUBSIDE SOON, BUT...
......
......

WE'RE LEAVING YOU HERE.
REST QUIETLY, OKAY?

バタン
BATAN (SLAM)

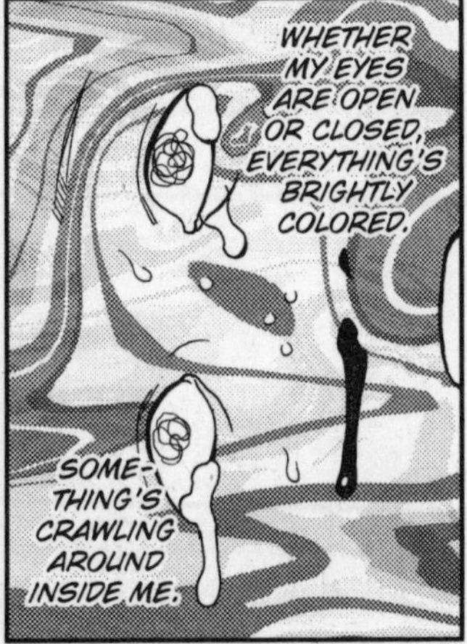
WHETHER MY EYES ARE OPEN OR CLOSED, EVERYTHING'S BRIGHTLY COLORED.
SOME-THING'S CRAWLING AROUND INSIDE ME.

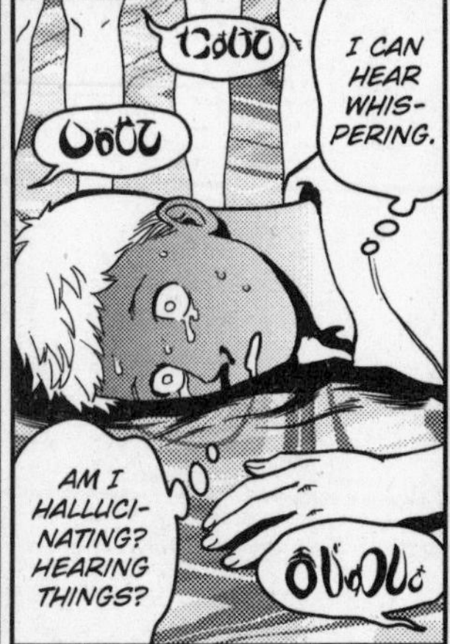
I CAN HEAR WHIS-PERING.
AM I HALLUCI-NATING? HEARING THINGS?

MANA SICK-NESS...
...BITES.

THE ROAD IS CHANGING OVER THERE.
HMM.

ガコ
GAKO (CLUNK)
ガコン
GAKON

ZU ZU
ズ ズ…
WE NEED TO OBSERVE A BIT MORE.
NOT BEING ABLE TO PROGRESS MUCH HURTS, BUT...

ズ
ZU (RUMBLE)
I THINK I SEE A PATTERN...
...OR MAYBE NOT...

ZU ZU ZU
ズ ズ ズ
THAT WAS CLOSE.
HA! HA! HA!
WE ALMOST GOT STUCK HERE.

ZU ZU ZU
ズ ズ ズ
THE GROUND IS RISING!
GET DOWN! GET DOWN!

ZU ZU
ズ… ズ…
HM?

ZUN (BOOM)

DO (STOMP)
YAAAAAGH!
DO
DO

IT LOOKS LIKE A BASI-LISK.
COCKA-TRICES ARE A HUNDRED TIMES WORSE!
WHAT-EVER YOU DO, DON'T GET BITTEN!
YOU'LL TURN INTO A STATUE.

DOOR ON THE LEFT!
GET INSIDE!

BAN (SLAM)

......

GARIRI
(SCRITCH)
GARIRI

WHAT SHOULD WE DO?
THIS WON'T HOLD FOR LONG.
GATSU
(SCRATCH)
GORI
(SCRAPE)
COULD WE ESCAPE OUT THE BACK?

IF IT'S LIKE A BASI-LISK...
...IT'S PROBABLY SENSING OUR BODY HEAT.
LAIOS TRIVIA
THEY'RE CALLED PIT ORGANS!
MAKING A CLEAN, QUIET GETAWAY WILL BE TOUGH.

...STILL, THAT'S THE SNAKE HEAD'S ABILITY.
GARI
THE BIRD HEAD WILL BE RELYING ON SIGHT.
JII
(STARE)

MAR-CILLE.
YOU REMEMBER HOW WE BEAT THE BASILISK, RIGHT?

......
......
LISTEN, YOU...

UUU...

NO MATTER WHAT, DON'T FLINCH!
THROW YOUR BODY AND SOUL INTO INTIMIDATING YOUR OPPONENT.
THAT'S EASY FOR YOU TO SAY.

MAKE YOURSELF LOOK BIG.
YES, I AM THE TALLEST ONE OF US...
...BUT THE ENEMY'S TWICE AS BIG AS LAST TIME.
KOSO (SNEAK)
こそ
KOSO
こそ

KOSO
こそ...
YELL AS LOUDLY AS YOU CAN.
I'M BAD AT YELLING.

COULD I HIT IT WITH AN EXPLOSIVE SPELL?
GARI (SCRATCH)
ガリ!
GARI
ガリ...
FROM HERE, THE ANGLE'S NOT...

HUH!?
WHAT WAS THE YELL? "WAAH"?
OR WAS IT "GRAR"?

IT'S "BRAWK"!
"BRAWK"!
WELL, WHATEVER.
I JUST NEED TO MAKE THE ENEMY RECOIL!

だ
DA
だ
DA
だ
DA
(TAP)
WAAAAAAAGH!!

ちらっ
CHIRA
(GLANCE)

パク
PAKU
(CHOMP)
THE END

AGH! THIS WON'T WORK!
SHEER ENTHUSIASM WON'T BE ENOUGH HERE!!!
I'M ABSOLUTELY GOING TO MESS IT UP!

I CAN'T DO WHAT LAIOS DID.
WHAT SHOULD I DO?

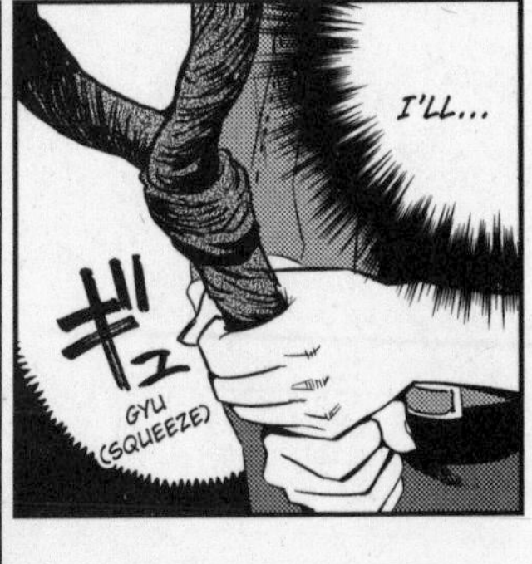
I'LL...
ギュ
GYU
(SQUEEZE)

I'LL DO IT MY WAY!

TO
(TMP)

だん!
DAN (STOMP)
ばん!
BAN (BAM)
ドオ
DOOON (BOOOM)
THE MOST TALENTED GIRL IN THE HISTORY OF THE SCHOOL—
MARCILLE

RAAA

WHAT WAS THAT EXPLOSION?

IT'S MARCILLE! WE'RE GOING IN!

!?

GARI (SLASH)
PUSHU (SPLURT)
RGH!
TOO SHAL-LOW!
HUH!?
HUH?
OH NO... I STOOD OUT TOO MUCH.
BOTH HEADS ARE FOCUSED ON ME!?
CHANT!
I WON'T MAKE IT—

SHA (SHWIP)

DOKURI (BADMP)
GHK...
BO (BWOOMF)

GO (THUNK)
GURAA (TOTTER)

ZUN (WHUD)
GA (WHAK)
GA
MAR-CILLE!
BATA
BATA (KICK)

YOU GOT BIT!?
I'M... FINE...

ZUPU (SHLUNK)

YOU DID GET BIT! YOU MORON!
FOR THE LOVE OF...

HERE. CLIMB ON.
SORRY.
LET'S GET BACK TO LAIOS.

I'M SORRY... I'M HEAVY, AREN'T I? ARE YOU OKAY?
NO, YOU'RE LIGHT.
BUT...

...WHAT IF YOU GET HEAVIER AND HEAVIER AND CRUSH ME?
HRNNNH
YES, THERE IS A MONSTER LIKE THAT.

HUH!? A COCKATRICE BIT YOU!?
THAT'S AWFUL!

OH.
WELCOME BACK...
DO YOU KNOW HOW TO DEAL WITH COCKATRICE BITES?
THERE'S A WAY?
I'LL TEACH YOU RIGHT NOW!

FIRST, TAKE OFF YOUR TROUSERS.
YOUR UNDERWEAR CAN STAY ON.

HAH!
HAH!

SIT ON THE FLOOR, PUTTING AS MUCH SKIN AGAINST SKIN AS POSSIBLE.
HFF...
HFF...

PULL IN YOUR ARMS. COVER YOUR EARS.
CLOSE YOUR MOUTH.

YES...
RIGHT.

GOOD...

NOW YOU CAN PETRIFY ANYTIME.
IT'S NOT A WAY TO AVOID PETRIFYING!?
BALLING UP AS TIGHT AS YOU CAN MAKES YOU MORE DURABLE.

BISHI (KRIK)

BISHI

BISHI

BISHI

AH! AWWW...
MIGHT BREAK
MIGHT BREAK
MIGHT BREAK
SHE HARDENED IN A REALLY UNSAFE POSE!!

SHE'S UNBALANCED TOO. SHE COULD TIP OVER ANY SECOND.
A SAFE, STURDY POSE
WE BLEW IT!

SO WHAT DO WE DO ABOUT THIS?

NOBODY WOULD WANT TO END UP LIKE THAT.
UMM...
WAYS TO UNDO PETRIFICA-TION?
THERE ARE A FEW.

FIRST OPTION, JUST WAIT FOR IT TO HEAL.
PETRIFICATION IS MORE LIKE A CURSE THAN A VENOM.
ELVES HAVE STRONG RESISTANCE TO MAGIC, SO THEY SHOULD RECOVER FASTER THAN OTHER RACES.

THE SECOND IS DEPETRIFICATION HERBS.
THAT, OR FIND OTHER ADVENTURERS WHO HAVE A CURE.

FINALLY...

...I'LL DO MY BEST TO CHANT THE TREATMENT SPELL.

YOU!?
MARCILLE TAUGHT ME THE BARE BASICS OF HOW TO READ A GRIMOIRE.
THERE SHOULD BE A DEPETRIFICATION SPELL IN HERE.

HRNNN...

WELL, LET'S LOOK FOR HERBS AND ADVENTURERS...
...AND STAY OPTIMISTIC ABOUT THE OTHER TWO IDEAS.

HOW LONG WOULD NATURAL HEALING TAKE?
FOR A TALL-MAN, ANYWHERE FROM SIX MONTHS TO TEN YEARS.
............
I'LL GO HARVEST THAT COCKATRICE.

THEY DIS-COLORED A LOT IN JUST ONE NIGHT.
THEY MUST SPOIL QUICKLY.

I NEED TO USE THEM UP FAST.
ザク ZAKU
ザク ZAKU (CHOP)
MAYBE I'LL PICKLE 'EM.

SHE'S TILTED. THAT DOESN'T LOOK SAFE.
THE TREMORS WILL KNOCK HER OVER.

SHOULDN'T WE PUT SOMETHING UNDER HER REAR?
YEAH, YOU'RE RIGHT.

I HAVE A GOOD IDEA!

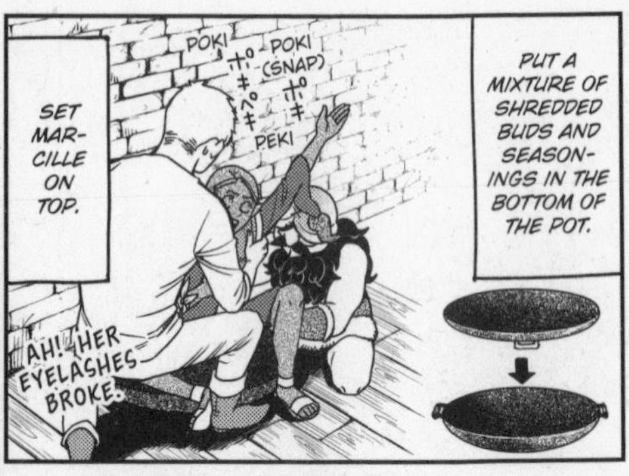
PUT A MIXTURE OF SHREDDED BUDS AND SEASONINGS IN THE BOTTOM OF THE POT.
POKI POKI (SNAP)
PEKI
SET MARCILLE ON TOP.
AH! HER EYELASHES BROKE.

SOAK COCKATRICE MEAT IN SALT WATER...
...SET IT ON MARCILLE'S LAP, AND...

ENSHRINED

HM... WELL.
SHE DOES SEEM MORE STABLE.
THIS WAY, SHE WON'T FALL OVER.
SHE LOOKS LIKE A HERETIC IDOL.

DAY ONE
AFTER THAT, LAIOS AND THE OTHERS WORKED VERY HARD...
DAY TWO
FOUND ONE...!!
OR DOES IT JUST LOOK LIKE ONE?
DAY THREE
HOW DO YOU USE IT?
IT SHOULD PROBABLY BE REFINED OR COMPOUNDED, BUT...
...WANT TO TRY STICKING IT ON HER?
...AND TRIED ALL SORTS OF THINGS.

DAY
FOUR

AM I PRONOUNCING THIS RIGHT?

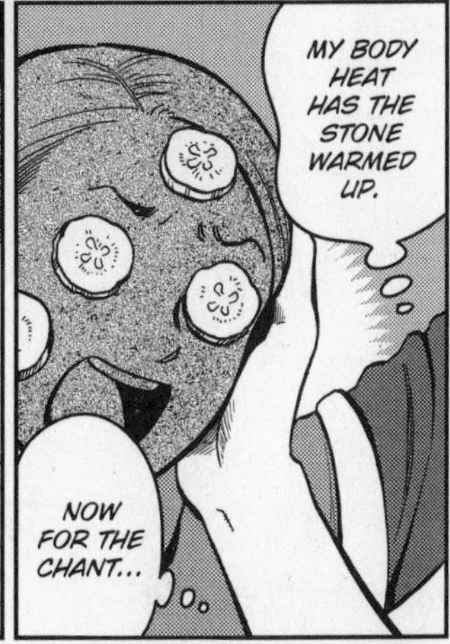
MY BODY HEAT HAS THE STONE WARMED UP.
NOW FOR THE CHANT...

ギョッ
GYO (SHOCK)
!?
LOOK OU...

ぐら
GURA (LURCH)

CHIRA (PEEK)
ちら

...HUH?

MAR-CILLE ...!!
YOU'RE SOFT!!

SUCCESS!
YAAAY!
HUH? HUH?
WHAT!? WHAT'S GOING ON!?

WHY THE VEGE-TABLE SLICES !?
WHY THE POTS!?

LET'S SEE.

......

THIS IS A SUCCESS TOO!!
SERI-OUSLY, WHAT!?

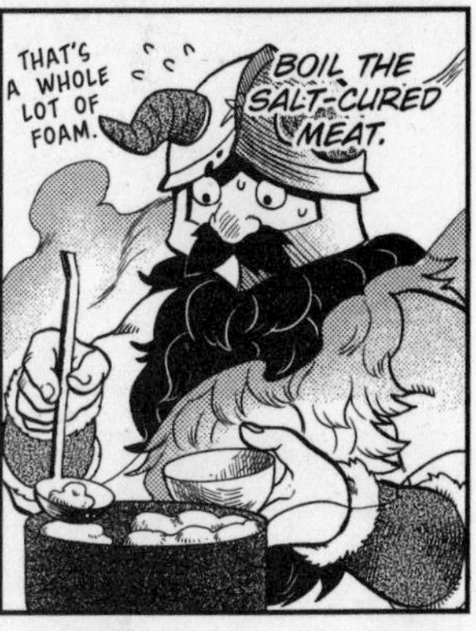
BOIL THE SALT-CURED MEAT.
THAT'S A WHOLE LOT OF FOAM.

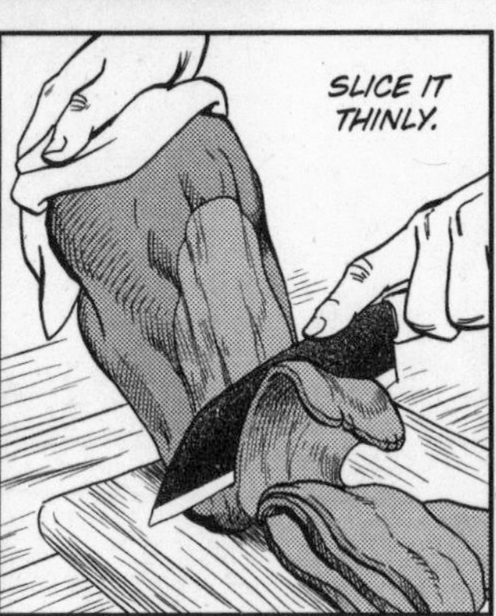
SLICE IT THINLY.

DRESS THE FERMENTED BUDS, AND...

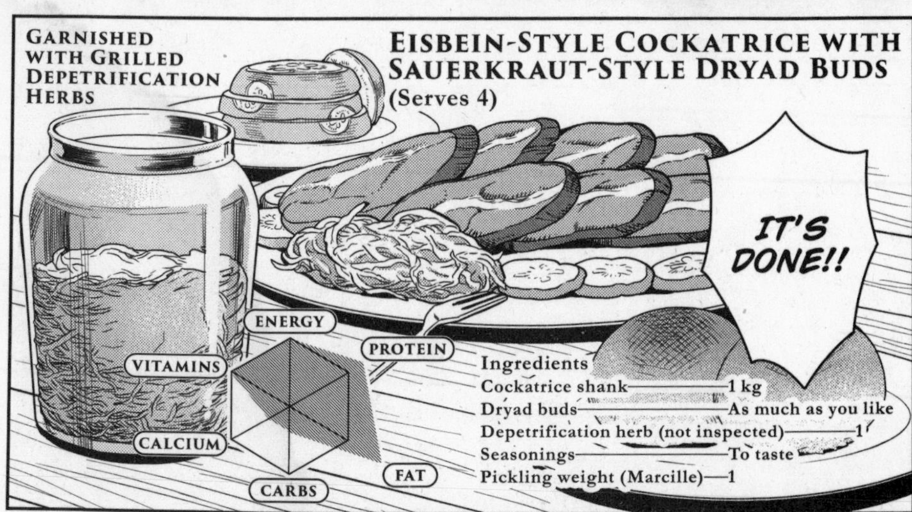
Garnished with Grilled Depetrification Herbs
Eisbein-Style Cockatrice with Sauerkraut-Style Dryad Buds
(Serves 4)
IT'S DONE!!
ENERGY
PROTEIN
VITAMINS
CALCIUM
CARBS
FAT
Ingredients
Cockatrice shank——1 kg
Dryad buds——As much as you like
Depetrification herb (not inspected)——1
Seasonings——To taste
Pickling weight (Marcille)—1

HUH?
IT'S BEEN THAT LONG!?

I CAST THE RESISTANCE SPELL AS SOON AS IT BIT ME...
THE VENOM STILL WON, HUH?
I WONDER WHAT DID WORK IN THE END.
WE TRIED SO MUCH, THERE'S NO WAY TO KNOW.

I HOPE IT WAS MY SPELL.
NAH.
I BET IT'S BECAUSE THE MEDICINAL HERBS WERE SO FRESH.
COULD THE PREPARED COCKATRICE MEAT HAVE NEUTRALIZED THE CURSE?

I CAUSED THEM TROUBLE, AND AT A TIME LIKE THIS.
I'M SOR—

AH!
NO. NOT THAT.
RIGHT NOW...

...THERE'S SOMETHING ELSE I SHOULD BE SAYING.
HWOO...
YES. FIRST AND FOREMOST...

DO NOT...
...USE PEOPLE AS PICKLING WEIGHTS.

Chapter 34: The End

35. Cleaners

WHILE YOU PEOPLE WERE MESSING AROUND...
...TURNING TO STONE, GETTING NOSEBLEEDS, AND HUNTING FOR FOOD...
...I'VE IDENTIFIED SEVERAL PATTERNS BEHIND THE CHANGES IN THE DUNGEON.

IT'S NOT AS IF I WANTED TO TURN TO STONE.
EXACTLY.
THAT WAS A PRODUCTIVE THREE DAYS.
YEAH, YEAH.

WHEN ONE PLACE IS BLOCKED, ANOTHER OPENS UP.
BASICALLY, THAT HAPPENS OVER AND OVER.
THE NUMBER OF DOORS, FURNITURE, AND BUILDING TYPES DOESN'T CHANGE.
HOUSES DON'T TURN INTO GRAVEYARDS.
BEHIND THAT HOUSE WE FOUND WITH SEVEN BATHROOMS, THERE MUST HAVE BEEN SIX HOUSES WITH NO BATHROOMS.

THE WALLS MOVE IN A CLOCKWISE SPIRAL AT SET INTERVALS.
THE STATUE POSITIONS ARE FIXED, INCLUDING THE DIRECTION THEY FACE.
BASED ON OTHER VARIOUS FACTORS...
OH!

CHIL-CHUCK, YOU'RE AMAZING !!
HEH-
WELL, THIS STUFF IS PART OF MY JOB.

CLEVER BOOTS!
YA LI'L GENIUS!
CUTIE!
...
BIG EARS.

I REMEMBER THIS STREET!
THAT'S THE HOUSE WHERE WE ATE THE DRAGON.

BUT THIS ROAD...
YEAH.

IT'S WHERE WE LOST FALIN.
ONLY A POOL OF BLOOD WAS LEFT.

FALIN IS THIS WAY!
RAH!
IF THEY SEE THAT BLOOD TRAIL, THEY'LL GET WORKED UP AGAIN.
HOW AM I GOING TO TALK THEM DOWN?

LAIOS, LOOK.
GIKU (FLINCH)

THAT'S...
UH, LISTEN, THERE'S A LOT TO BE CONCERNED ABOUT...
...BUT FOR NOW, LET'S...

...GO BACK TO THE... SURFACE...
...

HUH?
IT WAS HERE, WASN'T IT? THE DRAGON'S CORPSE?
IT'S BEEN CLEARED AWAY.
I'M SURE THAT CRACK IN THE WALL IS FROM WHEN THE DRAGON FELL, THOUGH.
IT'S ALMOST CLOSED TOO...

THE MAGI-CIAN'S EYES ARE COMING.

WAUGH!!
YEEP!
ZUSAA (JOLT)
DON'T YELL LIKE THAT!
I JUST SAW...
HUH?
MANA SICKNESS AGAIN, I GUESS.
AGAIN?
EVER SINCE THEN, EVERY SO OFTEN I HEAR THINGS.

YOU HEAR THINGS? I'M NOT SURE THAT'S MANA SICKNESS.
WHAT DID YOU HEAR?
"THE MAGICIAN'S EYES ARE COMING."
THE MAGI-CIAN'S EYES...
YOU MEAN—
ばっ
BA (TURN)

パタタ...
PATATA (FLUTTER)

...WING-BEATS!
ONE OF THOSE SMALL WYVERNS !!
WE HAVE TO HIDE.
NO, WE CAN'T.
THIS PLACE IS TOO OPEN.
C'MON, MARCILLE, WE'RE RUNNING!
...NO.
WE'LL HIDE ...
HUH?
...IN THE WALL!!
BWFF!
BITTAN (SMACK)
BATA (KICK)
JITA (FLAIL)
JITA
COME ON, YOU TWO! HURRY!
OKAY...
WHAT'S THIS...?
MORE MAGIC, HM...?
PATA (FLUTTER)
...

PATATA
DOBAA (BLORP)
BWAAAAH!
BLEHHHHH!
MARCILLE, WHAT WAS THAT SPELL?
DERO (OOZE)
HAFF... HAFF...
HAKH...
BOTA (PLOP)
...

......CLEANERS?
WHAT?

DUNGEON CLEANERS.
THEY'RE CREATURES THAT CLEAN UP DEBRIS IN THE DUNGEON AND REPAIR PLACES THAT GET DESTROYED. RIGHT?
THAT'S RIGHT.
I THOUGHT IT PROBABLY WASN'T SET COMPLETELY YET.

SAWA (FEEL)
さわ
SAWA
さわ
THIS PART IS THE OLD WALL...

...AND THE CLEANERS START HERE!
MUNI
むに
MUNI (SQUISH)
むに

THE FLOOR TOO!
LOOK. THEY'VE EVEN RECREATED WEAR FROM AGE AND FINE SCRATCHES.
YOU CAN'T TELL WHICH IS WHICH BY SIGHT.

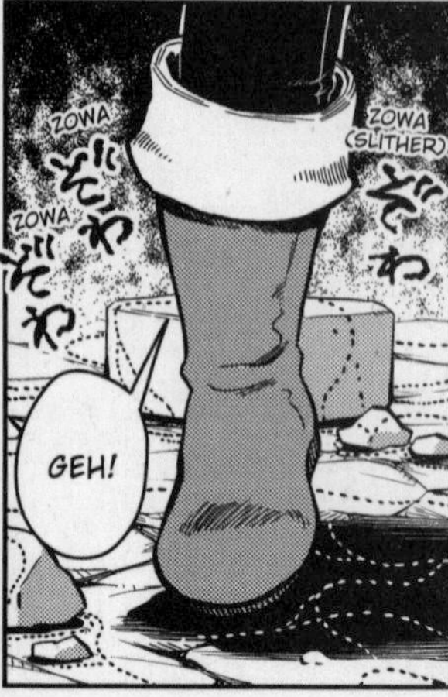
ZOWA (SLITHER)
ぞわ
ZOWA
ぞわ
ZOWA
ぞわ
GEH!

THERE ARE TINY THINGS CRAWLING ALL OVER THE FLOOR!
GROSS!

THEY'RE ALL CLEANERS.
A DUNGEON WITHOUT THEM WOULD COLLAPSE RIGHT AWAY.
THEY'RE NOT MONSTERS. THEY'RE HARM-LESS.

NO, THEY'RE NOT. THESE CRITTERS CHEW ON MY TENT A LOT.
HA HA.

WELL, THEY BREAK DOWN ANYTHING THEY THINK IS IN THE WAY.
SHOO!
SHOO!
THEY PROBABLY CAME TO EAT THE DRAGON'S CORPSE AND THE RUBBLE FROM THE EXPLOSION.
EEEK!

WHEN EXPLOSIONS DAMAGE THE DUNGEON, THEY APPEAR.
THEIR SECRETIONS PREVENT COLLAPSE AND KEEP FIRES CONTAINED.

THEN THEY START TO EAT THE GARBAGE IN THE AREA.
THEY AREN'T PICKY. THEY'LL EAT ANYTHING, ORGANIC OR NOT.

FINALLY, THEY SECRETE A LIQUID THAT FILLS IN MISSING PIECES...

...RETURNING THE DUNGEON TO ITS ORIGINAL FORM.

DONE.

IT'S THE SAME WAY LIVING THINGS HEAL.
CLEANERS AREN'T UNLIKE OUR IMMUNE SYSTEM, DESIGNED TO GET RID OF UNWANTED BACTERIA.
WHO ARE YOU CALLING "BACTERIA"?

THAT'S DUE TO MAGIC TOO?
AMAZING, ISN'T IT?

FOR CRIPES' SAKE... WHAT'S NEXT, A MAGIC DIGESTIVE SYSTEM?
IN THAT CASE, I WONDER WHAT THE DUNGEON WOULD EAT.
HA HA!

I'M LUCKY THAT BLOOD TRACK'S GONE.
PHEW...

LET'S GO BEFORE IT CHANGES AGAIN.
RIGHT.

STAIRS!
HAAAH...
WE'LL FINALLY BE ABLE TO GET OUT OF HERE.

THEN LET'S START GETTING PREPPED WHILE WE'RE HERE.
AH!
YES, LET'S GET THINGS READY FOR THAT.
"THAT"...
I SEE... "THAT," HUH?

DON (BAM)

DODON (BA-BAM)

DOOON (BOOOM)

HUH!? BY "THAT," YOU MEANT EAT!?
BEFORE CLIMBING A LONG STAIRWAY, WE SHOULD BUILD UP OUR STRENGTH.
I DOUBT THERE ARE TENTACLES ON THESE STAIRS.
SAY THAT SOONER!!
YOU ACTUALLY LIKE THAT THING, DON'T YOU?
OKAY! FOOD.
FOOD.
I DO NOT!

HM. WE HAVE SO MANY INGREDIENTS, I DON'T KNOW WHAT TO MAKE.
...MAYBE I'LL USE THAT.

COOK SOME GRAIN.

IS THAT THE STUFF WE FOUND ON THE THIRD FLOOR?
WE HAD SOME LEFT?
I KEPT IT IN RESERVE FOR WHEN OUR FOOD WAS GONE.

CHOP UP GROUND COCKATRICE MEAT, DRYAD FRUIT, MANDRAKE ROOT AND LEAVES, AND THE LEAVES OF THE DEPETRIFICATION HERB(?).
SEASON, THEN SAUTE.

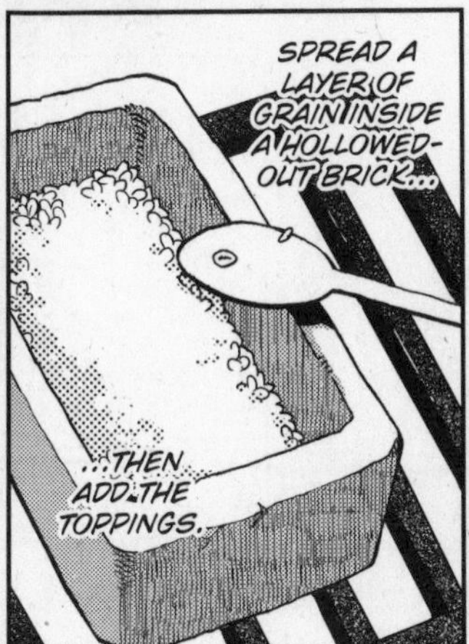
SPREAD A LAYER OF GRAIN INSIDE A HOLLOWED-OUT BRICK...
...THEN ADD THE TOPPINGS.

HEAT IT, BRICK AND ALL.

THEN...
NYUUU (ZLOOP)
BIKU (FLINCH)

HUH!? WHAT IS THAT THING!?
A COCKATRICE EGG.
I BROUGHT IT ALONG, BUT IT'S AWKWARD TO USE.
DOROO (GLORP)

FINALLY, ADD EGG SAUCE, AND...
TOROO (POUR)

IT'S DONE!!

## Cockatrice Stone-Baked Mother-and-Child Dish with Starchy Sauce

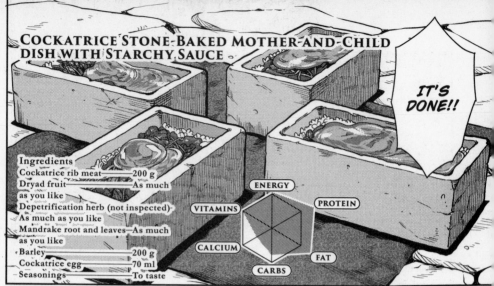

Ingredients
Cockatrice rib meat——200 g
Dryad fruit——As much as you like
Depetrification herb (not inspected)—As much as you like
Mandrake root and leaves—As much as you like
Barley——200 g
Cockatrice egg——70 ml
Seasonings——To taste

ENERGY
PROTEIN
FAT
CARBS
CALCIUM
VITAMINS

WOW, WHAT IS THIS? IT LOOKS REALLY GOOD.
IF MY PETRIFICATION HAD WORN OFF A LITTLE LATER, WOULD THEY HAVE USED ME TO MAKE THIS?
ドキ ドキ
DOKI (BADMP) DOKI
THE SCORCHED GRAIN IS DELICIOUS.

TRY STICKING YOUR SPOON INTO THE DISH.
HM?
MUNYU (SQUISH)
ムニュ
I USED BRICKS MADE OF DUNGEON CLEANERS.
SO WE CAN EVEN EAT THE DISHES!?
BLEH.


## Stone-Baked Dish
(Serves 1)

Ingredients
Dungeon cleaner secretions

THANK YOU, SENSHI!!
PAKKUN (CHOMP)
ぱっくん
...HOW DOES IT TASTE?
MY FIRST IMPRESSION IS "DIRT."
FURTHER ASSESSMENT PUTS IT CLOSER TO A MAGICAL MIXTURE OF GREEN CATERPILLARS, IRON, AND LEMON...
YOU'RE COMPARING IT TO ALL SORTS OF OTHER THINGS.

THERE'S JUST NO WAY TO DESCRIBE IT.
JYORI
じょり
じょり
JYORI (CRUNCH)
YOU SURE YOU SHOULD BE EATING MAGICAL CREATURES?
YOU'LL HEAR THINGS AND GET NOSE-BLEEDS AGAIN.

I WONDER WHAT THOSE HALLUCINATIONS ARE.
UMM...
WHEN WE GET BACK TO TOWN, YOU NEED TO SEE A DOCTOR ASAP.
A SHRINK.

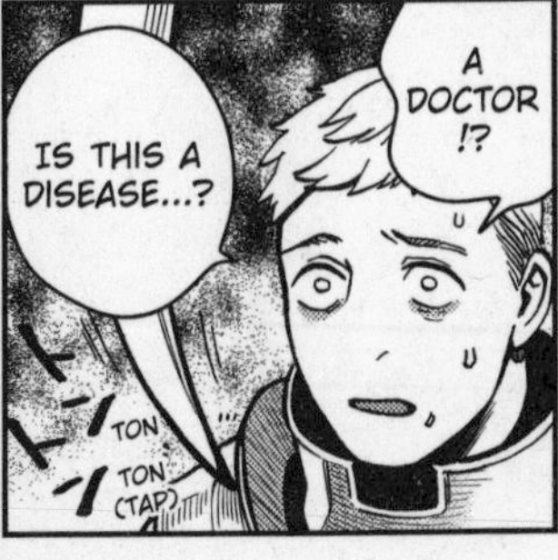
A DOCTOR!?
IS THIS A DISEASE...?
TON TON (TAP)

HM?

HMMMMMM!!?
I...
UH, ACTUALLY...
I SEE IT.
GURU GURU (TWIRL)
グル グル
HUH!? AM I HALLUCINATING THIS TOO!?
CAN THE REST OF YOU SEE IT!?
...WE'RE UNDER ATTACK!

GIRI (SQUEEZE)
GIRI
GIRI
ギリ ギリ ギリ……
GHK...

TSUU (SHF)
つっ…
GH...

HM?
WHAT'S THIS? FROG SKIN?

THESE HORNS ARE JUST PART OF THE HELMET.

A CHILD...

HFF. HFF.
HMPH.
SOME DEMONS CAN LOOK HUMAN.

THEY MAY SHOW THEIR TRUE NATURES...
...IF WE KILL ONE...

STOP IT, MAIZURU.

...I KNOW THEM.

......!
SHURO!!

WHAT'S A SHURO?
IT'S PROBABLY YOUNG MASTER TOSHIRO.
TOSSHURO...

WOW! SHURO! IT'S BEEN FOREVER!
びったん
BITTAN (FLOP)
IMAGINE MEETING YOU HERE! IT'S GREAT TO SEE YOU.
びったん
BITTAN
HAVE YOU LOST SOME WEIGHT?
TCH!

ピタ
PITA (STOP)

THANKS, SHURO!
SURE.
WELL, I NEVER! THE NERVE!
YOU LOOK LIKE YOU'RE DOING WELL. I'M GLAD.

BI (SLASH)
WHOA!
BARA BARA (FLUTTER)

SHURO'S A GOOD GUY WITH SERIOUS SKILLS.
HA! HA! HA!
HE'S ABOUT THE ONLY PERSON WHO'D CALL ME A FRIEND.

OH, LET ME INTRO-DUCE YOU.
THIS IS SENSHI.
HELLO.
SENSHI, THIS IS SHURO. HE USED TO BE PART OF OUR PARTY.

LET'S NOT STAND AROUND TALKING. WANT TO SIT?
WE WERE JUST EATING.

YOUR FRIENDS TOO. THEY CAN...
ZURARI (CROWD)
WOW! YOU'VE GOT A REALLY BIG GROUP!

...SAY, KABRU.
ISN'T THAT...?

IT'S GOOD TO MEET YOU...
YOU'RE LAIOS, AREN'T YOU?
MY NAME IS KABRU.

HM? YES, THAT'S ME.
IT'S NICE TO MEET YOU.

*To be continued...*

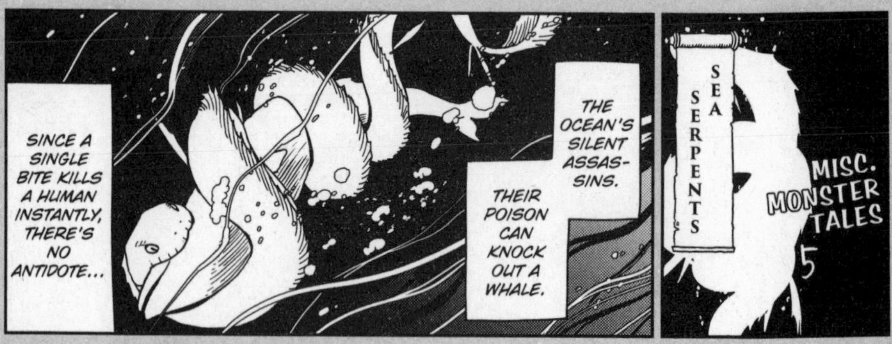
MISC. MONSTER TALES
5
SEA SERPENTS
THE OCEAN'S SILENT ASSASSINS.
THEIR POISON CAN KNOCK OUT A WHALE.
SINCE A SINGLE BITE KILLS A HUMAN INSTANTLY, THERE'S NO ANTIDOTE...

I'M GLAD NOBODY GOT BITTEN.
THAT WAS A CLOSE ONE.
KUROOO, I'M TIRED. CARRY M—
AAAAAH!
WHAT HAPPENED, KURO!? YOUR FACE LOOKS FUNNY!!

SOMETHING PRICKED ME.
HEY, YOU CLEARLY GOT BITTEN!!
WHAT DO WE DO!? IS KURO GONNA DIE!?
IF THE POISON WERE WORKING, KURO WOULD BE DEAD ALREADY.
KOBOLDS HAVE GOOD POISON RESISTANCE.

TH-THERE'S NO ANTIDOTE ANYWAY.
WE'LL JUST HAVE TO K-KEEP AN EYE ON IT.
WHY ARE YOU LAUGHING!?
LOOK WHAT HAPPENED TO KURO'S FACE!!
SNRK!
THE SWELLING LASTED FOR A WEEK.
IF OUR NINJA DOGS COULD TALK, LIFE WOULD BE SO MUCH EASIER.
UH-HUH.

DRYADS

LISTEN. BABIES DON'T COME FROM...
...KISSES OR CABBAGE PATCHES.
I KNOW THAT!!

PERFECT. I'LL USE THIS FLOWER TO EXPLAIN.

STA-MENS...
...OR "MALES," HAVE POLLEN.
WHEN THIS POLLEN REACHES THE STIGMA, A PART OF THE PISTIL, OR "FEMALE"...
I SAID, I KN—

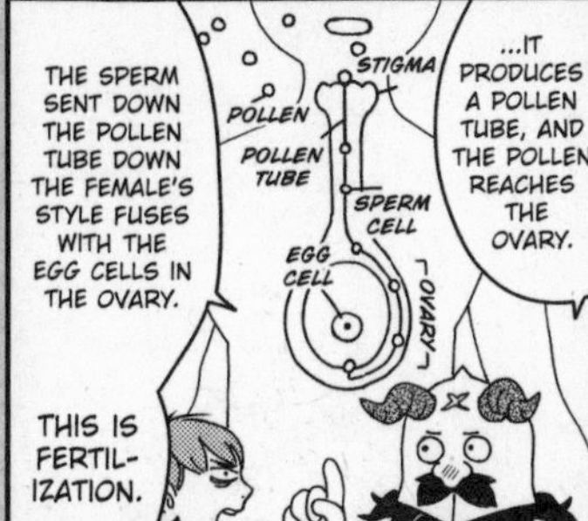
...IT PRODUCES A POLLEN TUBE, AND THE POLLEN REACHES THE OVARY.
STIGMA
POLLEN
POLLEN TUBE
SPERM CELL
EGG CELL
OVARY
THE SPERM SENT DOWN THE POLLEN TUBE DOWN THE FEMALE'S STYLE FUSES WITH THE EGG CELLS IN THE OVARY.
THIS IS FERTIL-IZATION.

THE FERTILIZED EGG CELL DIVIDES AGAIN AND AGAIN, AND THE OVARY BECOMES A SEED.
THIS IS THE FRUIT.

THE SEED GROWS UNTIL IT TAKES THE SAME FORM AS ITS PARENTS.
...AND SO LIFE IS HANDED DOWN.
NOW WE COME TO THE MAIN TOPIC.
WITH MAMMALS—

DRYADS POLLINATE BY KISSING.

I WAS EXPLAINING ONE STEP AT A TIME!
AAAAAH!
YOU RUINED IT!!

LIFE ...

I'M... NOT SURE.
THE CUT AND PREPARATION WERE DIFFERENT, SO I REALLY DON'T KNOW.
OH...

HM?
YOU KNOW. COMPARED WITH BASILISK.
WELL? HOW IS IT?

COCKATRICE

IT SAID THAT COCKATRICE TASTES LIKE STONE...
THE THING IS, IN MY FAVORITE BOOK, *THE DUNGEON GOURMET GUIDE*...
...THERE WAS A SECTION COMPARING THE TASTE OF BASILISK AND COCKATRICE.

HADN'T YOU ALWAYS WANTED TO COMPARE THEM?
......
......
...WHAT GIVES?

THAT'S...
THEN HE DIDN'T EAT IT.
IT SAID THAT KRAKEN TASTES GOOD ROASTED.

LATELY, THOUGH...
...I'VE STARTED TO THINK THE AUTHOR MAY NOT HAVE ACTUALLY EATEN ANY OF THOSE THINGS.
I'VE READ THAT BOOK SO MANY TIMES.

IT DIDN'T TASTE LIKE THAT TO ME.
YEAH ...
LIKE STONE?

...A LITTLE SALTIER THAN BASILISK.
I THINK MAYBE IT'S JUST...

READ ME MORE...
KOFF KOFF!
HYEH HEH!
OH NO...
WOW...
HAPPY BIRTHDAY!
NO!
I WANNA READ IT!
COPYING

HAAAH...
I SEE...

DUNGEON CLEANERS
THEY'RE BROADLY CALLED "CLEANERS"...
...BUT THEY EACH HAVE DIFFERENT PREFERENCES AND ACTIVE CONDITIONS.
APPROPRIATELY DISTRIBUTING THE TYPES BEST SUITED TO ANY PARTICULAR ENVIRONMENT IS ONE WAY TO SHOW YOUR DUNGEONIUM SKILLS!
THAT BEING THE CASE... THE AWESOME POWER OF THE LUNATIC MAGICIAN IS TERRIFYING.
I CAN'T BELIEVE SHE'S ABLE TO STABLY SUPPLY A SPACE THIS VAST.
BURU (SHIVER)
IT'S THAT BAD?
JUST THINK ABOUT IT!
BA (FWP)
TAKE A ROOM THIS SIZE. EVEN IF YOU WERE ONLY PLANNING TO FILL IT WITH SLIMES...
...FIRST YOU'D NEED TO ACQUIRE LAND THAT'S SUITABLE FOR A DUNGEON, AND THEN...
BARRIER EXPENSES
LIGHTING
TEMPERATURE REGULATION DEVICES
CONSTRUCTION EXPENSES
AIR FILTRATION SYSTEM
FEES FOR SUMMONING SPIRITS AND MONSTERS
THE TOTAL COST WOULD RUN YOU SEVERAL MILLION GOLD.

YES.
IN ALL LIKELIHOOD, THE LUNATIC MAGICIAN...
...IS FILTHY RICH!!
I'M SO JEALOUS!
THAT'S A PRETTY LOWBROW POWER.

# 5

# DELICIOUS IN DUNGEON

## RYOKO KUI

Translation: Taylor Engel Lettering: Abigail Blackman



Yen Press
1290 Avenue of the Americas
New York, NY 10104

Visit us at yenpress.com
facebook.com/yenpress
twitter.com/yenpress
yenpress.tumblr.com
instagram.com/yenpress

First Yen Press Edition: May 2018

Yen Press is an imprint of Yen Press, LLC.
The Yen Press name and logo are trademarks of Yen Press, LLC.

The publisher is not responsible for websites (or their content) that are not owned by the publisher.

Library of Congress Control Number: 2017932141

ISBNs: 978-1-9753-2644-9 (paperback)
978-1-9753-2685-2 (ebook)

10 9 8 7 6 5 4 3 2 1

WOR

Printed in the United States of America